9/99

WITHDRAWN

RACISM MATTERS

RACISM MATTERS

W. D. Wright

PRAEGER

Westport, Connecticut
London

Library of Congress Cataloging-in-Publication Data

Wright, W. D. (William D.), 1936–
    Racism matters / W.D. Wright.
      p. cm.
    Includes bibliographical references and index.
    ISBN 0–275–96197–4 (alk. paper)
    1. Racism—United States. 2. United States—Race relations.
  I. Title.
  E185.615.W78   1998
  305.8'00973—dc21   98–11134

British Library Cataloguing in Publication Data is available.

Library of Congress Catalog Card Number: 98–11134
ISBN: 0–275–96197–4

First published in 1998

Praeger Publishers, 88 Post Road West, Westport, CT 06881
An imprint of Greenwood Publishing Group, Inc.

Printed in the United States of America

The paper used in this book complies with the
Permanent Paper Standard issued by the National
Information Standards Organization (Z39.48–1984).

10 9 8 7 6 5 4 3 2 1

Contents

Contents

Preface

In a 1910 article entitled "The Souls of White Folk," W.E.B. Du Bois wrote: "The race problem is not insoluble if the correct answer is sought. It is insoluble if the wrong answer is insisted upon as it has been insisted upon for thrice a hundred years."[1] We are near the four hundreth year of the overall existence of America, going back to 1607 and the establishment of the first British colony, and the American people are still insisting on the wrong answer. Nearly four hundred years have gone by, and they are still looking in the wrong place for an answer. The wrong place, as a primary focus, is race, Black people, and the Black victims of race. Most white people prefer not to look at the matter in any form or search for an answer anyplace, and there is a reason for that. Whites have been the primary racists in America, and it is they who have primarily invested racism in America's history, culture, civilization, and everyday thinking and social interaction; they do not want to look in the mirror and engage in critical introspection.

But as contradictory and ironic as it sounds, most Black people, including most Black intellectuals, insist upon the wrong answer themselves and search in the wrong place for an answer; that is, they and other Blacks as the victims of what they, white people, and other Americans call race. It is not race, but rather *racism*, and the place to search for that right answer is white people functioning as racists. One can see why Whites do not want to look at or in any way touch this history or conjure up these memories and how they eagerly engage in denial, avoidance, and/or efforts to rationalize or justify their historical and continuing racist behavior. But another irony is that Black people, including Black intellectuals, let them get away with engaging in this kind of behavior, because they themselves do not focus thought or interest on racism and rarely talk about white people as racists or their historical and continuing racist behavior in the country.

And this contradictory, ironical, and abetting behavior continues. Just recently President Bill Clinton established a National Advisory Board on Race. This board has a number of prominent Black people on it, and these people, intellectuals and/or professionals, propose to join hands with white and other intellectuals and/or professionals to carry out a national discussion—a dialogue, as the president and his advisors insist—on race, meaning primarily Black people, primarily as the victims of race. The president and the board, therefore, are insisting on the wrong answer and will be searching in the wrong place for an answer. Even if it were argued that the president and his advisory board wanted genuinely to do something positive or significant to mitigate or end America's continuing debilitating malaise, the foregone conclusion has to be that they will do neither of these things, because they are not relating to the right subject in the first place, as a primary focus, which is White racist beliefs, thinking, social behavior, and abusive White racist power—which can only mean that they will not propose or help to implement national, regional, state or local programs that will significantly help them achieve their objectives. Second, their approach of focusing primarily on the wrong matter, race, and looking for answers in the wrong place, primarily the victimized lives of Black people (or other people of color) will only help to augment and keep alive in America the White racism that has always been and that continues to be the primary social malaise of the country, bringing detriment to Blacks and others in America, including many white people, as poor Whites can testify, and to America itself.

There are Black and White Americans, usually functioning in small groups, who are presently engaged in what they call *racial healing*. President Clinton and his advisory board on race talk of promoting this among Blacks and white groups in America, too. But this, again, is looking at the matter in the wrong way and looking for an answer in the wrong place. The problem in America has never been race, but rather racism—namely, the way white people have understood and related to race, either the white race or the black race, or other races of color. The way they have related to these races has been to glorify the white race and denigrate and punish all the others. Thus, White racism and *White racist divestment* are the places to look for the right answers. Focusing on these matters will require white people to engage in deep introspection that will lead, one hopes, to individuals divesting themselves of their own racism, that is, to self-alteration and self-healing. This will then lead to Whites eradicating racism from their families, from their social groups, from the institutions in which they function, and from the patterns of social interaction in which they participate. If the Black and white groups now meeting or forming in the country and the president and his advisory board on race can promote behavior like this among Whites, then there can be some serious people healing and bridging in America, and serious things can be done by the American people, by voluntary groups, and by their governments and other institutions to make life better—the way it is supposed to be in the country.

There are some personal reminiscences in this book, but it is primarily about white people and racism, with a discussion of what racism is, and how it differs from race. The mainline discussion is of white people believing, thinking, and acting as racists and using racist power in American history, and how these activities have affected and continue to affect American history, culture, and social life. I have dedicated this book to those white and other Americans who are not afraid to look at White racism and its creation, *White racist America*, and who can see the necessity of looking in these places for answers, and who want to free America from these old and continuing mephitic suppressants. I believe wholeheartedly that the future of America will be as bright and fulfilling as Americans honestly and actively intellectually, politically, socially, and morally seek to make it.

In closing, the terms *black* and *white* are treated in a special way in this book, representing my effort to provide a better understanding and to make better use of them. When the word *black* is spelled in lowercase, it refers to race or color. *Black* in uppercase refers to ethnic group, ethnic status, ethnicity, or community, that is, Black ethnic community. The Black ethnic group and the Black ethnic community are descendants of the Africans brought to this country as slaves between the seventeenth and nineteenth centuries, and their slave descendants. An individual designated as *Black* in this work refers to one who is a member of the Black ethnic group or the Black ethnic community. *Blacks* in plural refers to a few, many, or all Black people who are members of the Black ethnic group or the Black ethnic community. The phrases *black ethnic group* or *black community* refer to the color or racial attributes of the ethnic group or the ethnic community, but not references to culture or social life.

The word *white* receives similar treatment in this book. When lowercased, it refers to color or race. When uppercased, it refers to ethnic group, ethnic status, ethnicity, or community, that is, White ethnic community. White people form a large White ethnic group and ethnic community in America forged over the course of their history in the country. An individual designated *White* refers to one who is a member of the White ethnic group or White ethnic community. *Whites* refers to a few, many, or all White people who are members of the White ethnic group or White ethnic community. The phrases *white ethnic group* or *white community* refer to the color or racial attributes of the ethnic group or the community, but not references to culture or social life. White people in the Western world are part of Western civilization and, therefore, are part of a civilizational group and have a civilizational status. In this context, and in this book, the word *White* refers to an individual who is a member of this civilizational group. *Whites* refers to a few, many, or all White people who are members of this civilizational group.

Sometimes the words *white* and *Whites,* or *black* and *Blacks,* will appear in the same sentence or sequence of sentences. All this means is that I will be referring to white people, alternately, as a race or as an ethnic or civilizational group in the same sentence or sequence of sentences. It is similar to referring to America, alternately, by the words country or nation state in the same sentence or a sequence of sentences. The peculiar nature of the spelling of *white* and *black* in this book will inevitably cause some confusion. It contradicts the traditional spelling, which is long standing and widely known. However, I regard the traditional orthography as being inadequate, causing great problems for human identity in America. I believe it should be eradicated from public writing, and I hope to lead the way in achieving this objective through my own writings.

1.

History: What It Is, What It Tells Us

During the 1960s, I arrived at what I thought was a new, even revolutionary conception of history. My new view was that history should be understood as *human behavior in time and over time*. I had to overcome the reticence of my education and training as a professional historian to arrive at this conclusion. I had learned as an undergraduate history major and as a graduate student in history at the University of Michigan (and I could have learned this at any other institution in the country at the time) that history was *the past*, or was the *study of the past*. It had also been described as *change, transformation*, or a *process*. The descriptions had even seemed mysterious when history was referred to as an *art*, as a *social science*, and as a combination of *art and social science*. What I had never heard it explicitly called was *human behavior*. But, of course, in all the descriptions of history that I had heard or read was the implicit reference to human behavior, and always behavior of the past.

In the 1960s while I moved toward new conceptual ground, I discovered that part of the reason that historians did not have a clear conception of history was that they did not distinguish clearly and consistently between history as an academic discipline or methodology and history as subject matter or human reality. The word *history* covered—and obscured—both. Sociology studied society; political science studied government and politics. But the words in these examples showed a distinction between what was studied and who studied them. History was and is a monolithic word, an all-inclusive word, unclear and even confused about what it draws in. I ultimately saw very clearly that history had two realities that were distinctly different—but related. I was elated by my discovery, because now I had a way of looking at myself differently as a professional historian with what I thought was a more accurate perception. History as subject matter, as reality, was now clear to me. It was human behavior, but not just *past* human behavior. Human behavior went beyond the past. It began at some point in time and then continued over time. People died, but history continued. The behavior they initiated and participated in continued in generations removed from them. But how? That was the question. But I found an answer.

The way I discovered my answer was quite accidental. I had gotten my master's degree in modern European history at the University of Michigan. My special area of interest was Russian and Soviet history, which I taught in my first college teaching assignment at Buffalo State University College in Buffalo, New York. My course load also included a course in Western intellectual history and a general social science course. At that time Buffalo State did not separate the social science department into individual departments. Historians, political scientists, economists, sociologists, anthropologists, and psychologists all taught within the same department, and we were all required to teach a broad social science course in addition to our specialized courses. Five years later, the social science department gave way to individual departments, and I became part of the history department.

But it was the teaching of the general social science course that was the magical experience for me; it opened my eyes to what history was and what I should be teaching students: human behavior. I taught different forms of human behavior: political, economic, social, religious, and psychological. It wasn't long before the past, change, transformation, and process in my history courses became connected to people and their behavior. And I was now seeing very clearly how human behavior persisted beyond the point of its movement into time. The original behavior, or behaviors, were formed into ideals, traditions, customs, institutions, patterns of social interaction, and even into personality attributes. And these forms of behavior and personality attributes were passed onto others who assimilated, internalized, and used them and made them their own behavior and personality traits. They then passed the behaviors onto others who assimilated, internalized, and used them and made them their own, and who passed them onto others ad infinitum. This did not mean that change did not occur in history, in historical behavior, because it did. Ideals, political traditions, customs, and institutions, all manifestations of behavior, changed. Economic traditions, customs, and institutions changed. And social traditions, customs, and institutions changed. But change in historical behavior was usually slow because human behavior was structured or patterned and often had a religious or moral sanctity affixed to it that solidified it. This invoked guilt if attempts were made to change it—or made people cautious about changing their behavior. Personality attributes, formed by socialization and patterns of social interaction and by traditional, customary, and institutional behavior, also militated against change or instilled caution in attempting change. Social movements or revolutions, those forms of collective behavior, could bring about abrupt change, and in the case of revolutions, great discontinuities in human behavior. There would be new behavior that would be a sharp break with previous, manifested behavior. But for clarity an important distinction has to be made. There is the phenomenon of revolutionary change and the phenomenon of societal revolution. These are not the same realities. A revolutionary change puts something in place that has never existed before: an idea, an institution, a social practice, or an aesthetic form. A societal revolution, though, is a process of destroying a society and building a new one. The latter is more than just a process. It is something that involves people who voluntarily, but usually involuntarily, participate in the societal destruction and construction, being forced to engage in revolutionary behavior by revolutionary leaders and their power. Revolutions not only rip out cultural and social forms of behavior and replace them with others; they also rip out and replace psychological traits, causing much psychological distress and disorientation, until new traits can solidify and produce psychological and personal stability. Joseph Stalin understood this part of the Russian revolutionary process better than any of the other leaders, which was a reason he reincorporated manifestations of traditional Russian behavior in the revolutionary process, permitting people to grab hold of things they had once known, which were familiar to them, and which would give them psychological strength while they adjusted to racking changes and until new psychological traits could take root. Historians invariably interpret Stalin's return to Russian traditional behaviors as reactionary and fascistic politics and, in the case of some Marxists and communists, as a betrayal of the Russian Revolution. What Stalin was was a mass leader, and he understood mass psychology and put it to work on behalf of the Revolution. For instance, the new Soviet society was officially atheistic, and there were stringent efforts to destroy a belief in God, the Orthodox Christian religion, and the Russian Orthodox Church. Stalin recognized the large hole this put in Russian personalities, and so he endeavored to plug the hole with his cult of personality, making himself a god and having the Russian people worship him, as they did by the millions. Russian traditionalisms helped complete and consolidate the Revolution.

Over a period of five years at Buffalo State, I began looking at history as an academic discipline, and as subject matter or reality, from a broad social science angle. I learned, indelibly, that a historian had to have a broad and deep knowledge in several academic disciplines, or knowledge areas, that would broaden, deepen, and strengthen history as a research methodology and as an explanatory device. This broader and deeper conception of history as methodology and explanatory tool made it possible to see more in history, to investigate more widely, to ferret out more, to understand more. Namely, what? Human behavior, many manifestations of human behavior, that occurred in time and which could be viewed as continuing on in time long after the people had died who had put the behavior in existence.

All that I learned over five years was not always of clear benefit to students in my history courses. They were sometimes utterly confused about what was going on in my classes. They had signed up for history courses, but they were not always certain that they were learning about history. Sometimes they thought they were in a political science course, or a sociology course, or in a psychology course. Sometimes they also thought they were in a philosophy course, because I had learned a lot of philosophy, too, over those five years at Buffalo State from teaching Western intellectual history. I would raise philosophical questions in class for students to deal with, drawn from the subject matter we were studying and learning. I also raised social and psychological questions and issues in my history classes. I thought it was an exciting way to teach. Most of my students thought so too, as I judged from classroom participation, from what students said, and from what I heard from other faculty and administrators. I was very pleased to know that I was regarded as more than just a historian.

I actually became a historical sociologist. That was not a term I had at the time; I did not even know of such a term. I learned of it later, and even learned that historical sociology had at one time been a viable kind of historical methodology and orientation, coexisting along with the traditional canon, but one that had not held its place against the main orientation of professionally trained historians.

I learned, before I learned the concept of historical sociology, that William Edward Burghardt Du Bois (usually referred to as W.E.B. Du Bois) had been a historical sociologist; my later knowledge of the concept confirmed this. I became a disciple of Du Bois and, like him, a historical sociologist before I learned that that was what he had been and what I had become. Du Bois had been a socialist and at the very end of his life became a communist. But the latter was largely an appropriated name and identity, primarily an act of defiance on Du Bois's part against the American government that abused him and the Black people who had turned against him—people whom he had served hard and diligently and, at times, at great risk to himself, all of his life, since his early teenage years in the early 1880s in Great Barrington, Massachusetts. I did not follow Du Bois down his socialist or communist path. I knew too much about the history of Russia and the Soviet Union, totalitarianism, and Soviet life, and about communists in Eastern Europe and China to do that. I was in the 1950s and 1960s and am until this day a liberal democrat, knowing fully the difference between liberalism and democracy, but also their necessary relationship to form the philosophical or ideological and the practical—the cultural and institutional—basis for societal and human freedom. I was also, from the late 1960s to the present day, a Du Boisian scholar, specifically, a Du Boisian historical sociologist. Du Bois, as I later learned, combined history and sociology to study the life of Black people in America. He looked at Black social life historically and also viewed Black history sociologically, so that he could explain how Black cultural and social life came into existence, how it was perpetuated over time, and the specific forms that existed over time.

In the time between 1962 and 1967, when I was viewing history differently and was becoming a historical sociologist without conceptualization, I did not know much about Du Bois, or about any other Black historical figure, for that matter. I had heard about Frederick

Douglass, something about Booker T. Washington and Ralph Bunche, something about Marian Anderson, and, maybe something dimly, about Mary McLeod Bethune. But I was almost wholly ignorant of Black history. I knew a lot about Western European history, especially Russian and Soviet history. I had knowledge in various social science areas, but it did not include much about the culture, social life, and psychology of Black people in the United States. What I knew about being black and Black came from the experience of living these ways in America. I had no formal knowledge about either. I did not apply the social science analytical tools I learned to Black people. But I did before the 1960s were up, and all the years thereafter.

What made me change? Two things: the Black Liberation Movement going on at that time in the 1960s, and my knowledge that I did not know much about Black history, or formally, about Black culture and social life. But I did not know much about American history either and did not have much formal knowledge about American culture and American social life. I knew why I was formally ignorant about Black people and America itself. I did not learn anything about Black history or Black life in America in my public school education that I can recall. And I did not learn much about American history and American life either. When I attended the University of Michigan as an undergraduate and graduate student, no Black history courses were taught, and no sociology or other social science courses, that I recall, taught about Black people, their culture, community, and social life. Black people had no presence or visibility in the academic curricula at the University of Michigan—not to any appreciable extent anyway. In American history courses, there might be something said about them, in those courses that mentioned slavery. Michigan was not unique in its omission and neglect. These were realities to be found in what were then described as White colleges and universities, and which today would be called predominantly White colleges and universities in America, rather than the American colleges and universities that they are. If the terminology had existed back in the 1950s and 1960s, when I was an undergraduate and graduate student and someone had been inclined to use it, it could have been said as a form of criticism that the curricula at Michigan and other universities and colleges where white people were the overwhelming, dominant element were *politically correct*. This would have translated into the understanding that a White-dominated and oriented curricula was natural, normal, and correct. In the mid 1950s and up to 1962, when I attended the University of Michigan, most if not all the teachers were white. Most, and doubtlessly close to all courses in all academic departments that focused on people, focused on white people, either in America, Europe, or other parts of the world. This seemed the natural, normal, and correct focus. There was no fanfare about any of this, no conscious imposition of subject matter and orientation, no outburst of justifying rhetoric or ideological bombardment, and no glaring displays of power. There was no conscious effort to disparage other people or to be cruel to them. And any suggestion that this was an intention, or that this was happening, would not have been understood, would have been resented and assailed, and would have even been rebuffed with feelings of hurt that such thoughts or such a suggestion could be entertained.

At the University of Michigan and at other universities and colleges in America where white people had this overwhelming and dominant presence—as instructors, administrators, and students—there was a simple and direct understanding: there was essentially only one way to look at knowledge and truth, which was that white people had produced them; the knowledge and truth produced related to white people and was about them, their history, lives, and achievements; and that this truth and knowledge had to be learned by white people and all other people. Further, the knowledge and truth produced by white people, which related to and which was about them, were the keys to graduation from undergraduate and graduate school and for professional success.

I understood all of this during all the years I attended the University of Michigan. I had been invested with this kind of understanding by my public school education, which I took to Michigan, which enlarged upon it. What I had also learned and understood, by noninstruction, first in the public schools and then again at the university, was that Black people had never produced knowledge or truths. Both instances of noninstruction had told me that Black people had made no contributions to American history, culture, and social life, that, indeed, they had not even been significant participants in these realities.

I did not take any courses in American history at Michigan to see whether there was something to learn about what Blacks had contributed to America. All the other college courses I took seldom referred to Black people at all. I doubt that any American history course would have thrown any light on the subject. I actually shunned American history courses when I attended the University of Michigan. I did it deliberately. I did not want to learn anything about George Washington, Thomas Jefferson, Andrew Jackson, Abraham Lincoln, or any other important American historical figure, or about what white people had done in American history.

There was another reason I shunned and even fled from such courses and knowledge—although I would not have been able in the years I attended Michigan to explain and clarify my action. I did not have enough knowledge for that. I did not know enough about racism, what it was, how it functioned, how it affected people, Black and white, and how it had affected me personally. When I learned more about racism from studying it formally, making Du Bois's writings on racism the centerpiece of my study, I learned I had been affected by racism and the ways in which I had been affected. And looking back, I saw that White racist behavior had made me considerably anti-White, even though I had white friends, and had turned me off from wanting to learn about white historical figures and about what white people had done in American history.

Later, I would learn, from my study of racism in America, that white people and Black people were both alienated people in America, but in different ways. I learned that white people were more alienated than Blacks and that their alienation was accompanied by more serious psychological afflictions. This was a result of Whites being and acting as racists. Du Bois clarified this situation for me, and it's a good thing he did, because the writing on racism, which is vast, from the pens of Black and white commentators, says very little about how racism has affected white people in America. Indeed, the impression is that they have not been affected at all. Some sociologists have recently drawn attention to this great omission in the literature and discussions on racism.

> Racism in America is rooted deeply in the very structures of society. It is not solely, or even mainly, a matter of personal attitudes and beliefs. Indeed, it can be argued that racist attitudes and beliefs are but accessory expressions of institutionalized patterns of white power and social control. Moreover, racism in America is a white problem. It is a white problem not merely because of hostile reactions of minorities to overt expressions of white racism but because

racist attitudes, behavior, and social structures have direct
and indirect impacts on whites. . . . Contemporary social
thought has unaccountably ignored this fact. We have developed some awareness of racism's consequences for its
victims . . . and we recognize in general ways the imperfec-
tion of a social order in which racism flourishes. But just
what does racism do to white people?[1]

This was a question asked in the 1980s. Whites had been racists in
America for centuries, but it was only in the 1980s that some social
scientists thought it was pertinent to ask how the racism that white
people had promoted in America had affected them. Fortunately,
there had been Black people in America, usually individuals not acting
as social scientists, who had made evaluations. Frederick Douglass, as
I learned in my own later study of American history, Black history,
and White racist behavior in the country, was an individual who had
made an assessment. He wrote particularly on how the racism of
Whites affected their thought and psychological processes:

Self-deception is a chronic disease of the American mind
and character. The crooked way is ever preferred to the
straight in all . . . mental processes, and in all . . . studied
actions . . . [Americans] are masters in the art of substituting a pleasant falsehood for an ugly disagreeable truth, and
of clinging to a fascinating delusion while rejecting a palpable reality.[2]

The Americans that Douglass was talking about, of course, were
white Americans. White people at the time Douglass made his remarks did not regard Black slaves or nonslave Blacks as citizens of
the United States, or as Americans; thus, Douglass's remarks were
not a reference to Blacks. The abolitionist was a social philosopher,
as well as a social critic and political activist. He also had the ability
to analyze the intellectual and psychological attributes of people,
namely, white people, and specifically, their intellectual and psychological attributes in functioning as racists. He was generalizing in his
remarks, recognizing the way culture inculcated large masses of people with similar intellectual and psychological traits and behavioral
responses. He saw how the racist-inundated American culture and
social life interpenetrated the minds and personalities of masses of

white people, investing them with racist psychological attributes and
racist ways of perceiving and thinking. Psychologically, and as a consequence of being racist and inflicting themselves with their own racism, white people were prone to self-deception, were diminished in
their ability to introspect, and had a strong proclivity to deny reality,
especially social reality. Intellectually Whites, functioning as racists,
were prone to fanciful thinking to construct fantasies and regard them
as knowledge, truth, or factual representations, while denying or ignoring actual knowledge, actual truth, and actual representations.

Another Black person who had the ability and knowledge to analyze the impact of racism on the mind and personality of white people
was Du Bois. He showed the capability at a very young age, as a
teenager, long before he became an academic scholar. But in his very
first scholarly monograph in 1895, he made the following observation
of how the racism of white people had impacted their own mind and
psychology:

> We have the somewhat inchoate idea that we are not des-
> tined to be harassed with great social questions, and that
> even if we are and fail to answer them, the fault is with the
> question and not with us. Consequently we often congrat-
> ulate ourselves more on getting rid of a problem than on
> solving it.[3]

In his remarks, Du Bois referred, like Douglass, to the proclivity
of White racists to delude themselves and to deny and ignore reality,
especially social reality, and especially if it were an unpleasant social
reality. Du Bois also indicated that white people, functioning as racists, determinedly avoided unpleasant social reality. This made Whites
in America, as racists, strongly anti-intellectual, not necessarily in general, but certainly in certain areas of their lives. The implication is that
when Whites engaged in intellectual activity in social matters, and
especially troubling or unpleasant social matters, their intellectual responses would be rather inadequate. This kind of implied observation
could also be seen in Douglass's comments. Another important thing
that Du Bois noted, again by the implication of his remarks, specifically the comment "the fault is with the question and not with us,"
was that white people, as racists, had a strong compulsion always to
think of themselves as a guiltless and innocent people, and always
guiltless, innocent, and nonresponsible in regard to social problems,

having nothing to do with creating them or with maintaining them. But if white people did not have anything to do with creating and maintaining social problems, who did? Du Bois, in the above quoted comments, made no direct reference to white racists in an intellectual and psychological manner blaming their victims, but his remarks imply such a reference. Over the course of the years that he would write on the subject of racism, Du Bois would become explicit and more detailed about the intellectual, psychological, and numerous other ways that the racism of white people affected them and the ways their racist afflictions induced them to relate to other people and to America.

In the early 1960s, I felt a great pressure to learn about racism, beyond what my own experience in life had taught me or beyond what I had learned from other Blacks who had the same general experience. The Black Liberation Movement raging at the time and the observable White resistance to it were the great pressure. There was also my own involvement in this movement, which acted as a pressure. After I graduated with a B.A. at Michigan, I went to my home town and joined with other Blacks to fight the racism and segregation there. We had considerable success in our efforts. I returned to Michigan for graduate work, and also, off and on, got involved in liberation activities there, until I graduated with my master's degree. I did not make much of an effort to learn about racism in an academic manner, while getting a master's. I only nitpicked the literature on the subject. I might have been more interested and motivated to carry out this research and learning in a larger way if I had been interested in studying American history. I knew there was a connection between racism and that history. If I didn't learn something about White racism studying American history, I might have been able, had I learned more about racism itself, to fit it into American history myself. But I was still very turned off, despite the Liberation efforts I had participated in and was still participating in intermittently, to learn about white people in American history. My Liberation participations themselves might have turned me against delving academically into this subject. But in the end, my nit-picking with one subject and not being interested in the other could be charged to my need to take courses and study subjects that would get me my master's degree in modern European history and land me professional employment.

That occurred in 1962, when I was hired as an instructor at Buffalo

State University College. I had several courses to prepare for teaching. I had to learn a whole lot of new material in all of the different social science areas, which took an enormous amount of time. There was not much time for other things I was interested in, that the sights and sounds of the Black Liberation Movement in America kept me interested in. I nitpicked some more on the subject of racism at Buffalo State.

But in the end, after five years at Buffalo State, I had to make some momentous decisions. I had not done any work toward my Ph.D., and now I had to leave Buffalo State. But I was undecided as to what I should get my Ph.D. in. There was, in 1967, a very strong urge to get into Black history and American history, realizing I could not avoid these areas any longer. But on the other hand, I did not know of any college or university that was teaching courses in Black history. I heard there were some Black colleges and universities that did that, but I did not seek to confirm that because I was not going to go to any of those institutions anyway. I did not know of any that gave a Ph.D. in history. And it seemed inconceivable that any of the institutions gave a Ph.D. in Black history. Black students at many of the major U.S. universities and colleges were demanding Black history courses, which only meant that such institutions did not have them, much less a Ph.D. in Black history. A Ph.D. in American history could be obtained at any of these institutions, and a research area in Black history might perhaps be possible; in that one would be able to write a dissertation on some individual, group, or event in Black history. I decided I had to get a Ph.D. in American history and write a dissertation on someone or something in Black history.

But my decision was racked and became less firm. After I had made it, and when it was still my (and my family's) private decision, and not as yet known to members of the history department, one of my colleagues said to me that I should take an interest in what he called, and what it would have been called in those days, "Negro history." Since I had a master's in modern European history, my colleague's encouragement, logically, should have been to pursue a Ph.D. in that subject. If I had been white, that would have happened. But I was not white. And while my colleague never evidenced direct hostility to my teaching Western intellectual history and Russian and Soviet history, I knew there were members in the department, as there had been members in the broad social science department, who had some antipathy toward this, especially my teaching Russian and Soviet history. It was absolutely unheard of that somebody Black was doing that. I was a surprise to the people who hired me, but they did, and maybe because my being Black did not matter to them. This was also the time of the Black Liberation Movement, so there was a groundswell of Americanism, an inducement to be fair. Maybe it was moral integrity, Liberation, and American pressure together in combination that got me on at Buffalo State.

But there was also resentment, and I knew it, about my teaching Russian and Soviet history. At the opening of every semester, I saw surprised looks, confounded looks, and angry looks on the faces of students when they saw someone Black walking into class to teach them Russian and Soviet history. I still see such looks, as I still teach these subjects where I presently work. There was one person in the history department who really did not want me teaching Russian and Soviet history. But I do not think there was any racism involved in it, not any strong racism anyway. He was Polish, and those were also his specialized subject areas, and he wanted to teach those courses. But some members in the department did not want him to. One was always adamant about it, saying that because he was Polish, he would not be objective. I remember saying to him on one occasion when he made that kind of remark, that if that were so, then the Americans in the department teaching American history—and he was one of them—should not be teaching that subject. He never made such an absurd comment again in my presence.

And perhaps even my colleague who said I should go back to school and see what I could do in the way of studying "Negro history" and writing a dissertation in that area also meant well. There were demands for Black history and Black people to teach the courses. Maybe that had been his motivation. But all I could see at the time, at that moment, was a white man endeavoring to put me in my place, saying to me that white people taught the history of white people, whether it was in America or Europe. And that Black historians were to stay away from these areas, and in their own place, by teaching Black history. There were some historical and social pressures working on me in this situation, and I knew it. And I knew they were not all good. Those pressures worked on other people in the history department and social science department, too, and not in a good way. But this was America. And, in the end, this was why I knew I had to go back to school for a Ph.D. in American history, with a research and dissertation possibility in Black history.

Actually, and owing to a number of complications, I did not get my Ph.D. until a number of years later. I got it in American history and did a dissertation in Black history, doing it on the socialist analysis of W.E.B. DuBois. This was when I learned a great deal about this great man in Black history, American history, and world history. I learned that he was not only a socialist—and never, as some people still believe, a Marxist—but that he was also a sociologist, indeed, the progenitor of scientific sociology in America. He was also a historical sociologist. He was also the foremost analyst of White racist thought, psychology, and behavior in the United States. Indeed, that this country has ever produced. I also admire Frederick Douglass's capability in this area and would tell anyone who wanted to study White racism in America to start with these two men, who left a lot of critical and enlightened commentary.

I had to study racism on my own, which I did and have been doing since the 1960s. It was the Black Liberation Movement that told me that this just had to be done. It also made it clear to me that I had to study American history and Black history. So I had three broad subjects that I had to get into. They were all related. I knew that before I plunged into studying the three subjects. I just did not know how intertwined they were, and especially how deeply they were absurdly and mephitically intertwined. But I found out.

What I call my revolutionary conception of history proved to be of great value to me. It had already unstrapped me from the rigid canon of historical research, writing, and understanding, removing a whole lot of restrictions that are involved in going after knowledge as a historian. I looked at history, as subject mattter, as human behavior in time and over time. I knew how historians liked their documentary evidence, which I had a strong affinity toward, too—this part of the canon. But I knew that those documents, in order to be interpreted to the fullest extent, to draw out the reality to which the documents were referring, needed to be analyzed with the knowledge of psychology, sociology, cultural anthropology, or philosophy. Maybe psychological theory, or sociological theory, or political theory as well. The historical canon grudgingly opened to such aids. It usually placed social science and even historical theories in the category of problematics in historical research and writing, expressing fear that they would promote speculation, blur facts, or be substituted for facts. Those were some valid injunctions, but they could also function to

restrict or suppress historical thinking and imagination as well as produce a paralysis of intellectual effort in historical research and writing.

I knew my way of looking at history, from different academic angles, and as human behavior in time and over time, was going to help
me study racism. I was going to see that subject from various angles:
historical, cultural, social, psychological, or political. And I was going
to focus on the people who were the racists, who believed, thought,
and acted as racists, and also on the victims of racism. Into my research on this subject, I began to see how White racism impacted the
broad realities of American history, American culture, and American
social life. My multiangled and integrated approach to the study of
history and my philosophical view that historical reality was human
behavior in time and over time helped me to penetrate the interior
of these realities and to understand them.

History, as I concluded in the early 1960s, was the primal source
of human knowledge and understanding. It was the primal context
in which all other knowledge occurred, which helped to define that
knowledge, to make it intelligible, and to give it meaning. History,
as historical reality, indicated when things originated: knowledge,
traditions, customs, institutions—everything that occurred within the
historical context. It indicated how things were conserved or preserved, how they changed, how they were conserved or preserved by
changing. History, as reality, validated or invalidated things, legitimized them, or proclaimed their illegitimacy; offered the best basis
on which to make judgments of people and their actions. Historical
knowledge of human behavior in time and over time identified those
responsible for historical happenings, for initiating them, maintaining
them, or changing them. History as human behavior in time and over
time established and clarified what was important to people, what
mattered to them. These were the things that got locked into history,
into its institutions, its culture, and its social patterns, and into the
minds, personalities, and the behavior of people who participated in
these institutions and patterned realities. Finally, history, as historical
reality, as human behavior in time and over time, revealed the gaps
that existed between thoughts, beliefs, and the ideals of people and
their actual behavior. It therefore pointed to where the critical analysis
was to take place in historical research and the area from which the
best critical interpretation would be made in historical writings.
American history was made for such analyses and historical writings.
I knew that before I ever got academically into that subject and even

before I undertook my study of racism or of Black history. I already knew about that gap, and had known about it for years, all of my life, as had other Black people in America. But now I had plans to study it, the knowledge, truth, and realities of the gap, and I was excited about doing so.

2.

Racism Matters

When I contemplated studying racism in the latter 1960s, I was motivated initially to see if I could understand better than I did why white people at the time were showing such contempt and loathing for Black people and why they were gathered in mobs in the streets and engaging in such verbal and physical violence against them. I knew that what Black people were seeking was not wrong. They said they were seeking recognition of their human dignity, individual rights, equal rights, individual opportunities, equal opportunities, and justice. These things, as ideals and practices, constituted freedom in America. What Black people as well as other people in the country had always heard was American freedom, that America stood for freedom. So clearly, *America* was not against what Black people were seeking and indeed was encouraging them in their quest for freedom. White people kept asking Black people what they wanted—as it was usually said, "What do Negroes *want?*" Black people kept telling them what they wanted: freedom. And they spelled it out for them, their understanding of freedom in America. But these clarifications had little to no effect on most White people, because they kept thinking and asking the same wrong question. And they kept resisting the efforts of Blacks in their grand quest. Blacks, I saw then, were acting as Americans. And white people, as I saw then, were acting in an *anti-American* or *un-American* manner.

I recalled the Senate hearings on alleged communists in the American army in the 1950s, many of which I saw on television, seeing Senators Joseph McCarthy and John McClelland going after the defense counsel Joseph Welch and the defense witnesses opposite them. This whole thing was a spectacle, but a double spectacle for Black people. The Soviet and Eastern European communists and the communists in China were enemies of the United States to be sure. But we Black people knew that white racists were, too, and an even greater internal threat to America than the communists were or ever could be; we also knew how southern Whites, especially, were using the communist threat to cloak their own racist power and racist threat to the country. I was to learn later in my study of Black history and American history that Black people had had a lot to do with diminishing the communist threat to America. In the 1930s the Soviet communists, with their followers in America, had endeavored to win masses of Black people to their cause. Save for some individuals, most Blacks rejected their recruiting and propagandistic efforts. In the 1930s, Black people went headlong into the Democratic party, became part of the new urban coalition centered in the northern part of the country, and lined up fully and loyally behind America. The people the Soviet and American communists thought were the most disenchanted, dispirited, and most manipulative people in America and the most useable and sacrificial (these Whites showing their own racism) found out that Black people were not what they thought. What Blacks did, showing their independence of mind and their affinity and loyalty to America, broke the back of the combined foreign and domestic communist effort to make their cause a serious and widespread one in America. America had a friend in Black people. Blacks, former slaves, subject to racism and segregation and unrelenting abuse, but still loyal and supportive of America, represented a national treasure, a national resource of moral and spiritual strength and regeneration.

These were traditional Black strengths and realities in America, traditional primordial sources for America's refurbishment, for America's self-image and justification. These realities also profoundly disturbed white people, who could not understand this Black behavior, could not understand from whence it came. It was entirely too mysterious for them. But the genuine quality of it that they perceived made it a real thing that they had to contemplate. They did, but with fear and anger, maybe with thoughts and feelings of being less superior, perhaps with shame. But Whites would not permit any of the humbling perceptions to stay alive long. They would be too threatening, too disorganizing of mind and personality. Such perceptions, like the people who provoked them, had to be deflected or suppressed.

Looking back on the 1960s, and remembering Whites in the streets and the way they were and what they were doing to Blacks, who themselves were doing America's bidding and showing loyalty to it and what it stood for, I thought that many Whites were perhaps hostile or violent toward Blacks to silence their own inner exposures and fears. Blacks could not be more American than they were. But the truth was, they were. Whites had asked Black people over and over again what they wanted. If they had been as American as they thought or claimed they were, they would have known. If they had not been the racists they were, they would have known and would have known why Blacks themselves were out in the streets and were making the demands they were. I could see looking back, and knowing more about American history, Black history, and White racism, that White feelings of guiltlessness, innocence, and nonresponsibility functioned infectiously among Whites in the 1960s.

My research on White racism in America actually plunged me into an intellectual quagmire that took me years to get out of and to gain an understanding of what racism itself was. The quagmire was simply that the literature on racism by historians, social scientists, and others was about race and writing on such things as prejudice, race prejudice, racial discrimination, or racial segregation. And the word *racism* was also used. This word actually threw confusion into my research on racism. And this is what plunged me into the intellectual entanglement. And studying Du Bois on racism did not help me out—not right away, and not for years.

Du Bois did not use the word *racism* very often, and only over the last years of his life. He most often wrote about race, race prejudice and, most often, about race prejudice toward the black race or Black people. Du Bois also used other words like *white supremacy, caste, color caste,* and *color discrimination.* Not initially, but eventually, I found the phrase *white supremacy* troublesome. I also found the phrase *white racism,* or *White racism* troublesome. These were phrases that others writing on racism often used. But such people also used phrases like *race, race prejudice, racial prejudice,* or *racial discrimi-*

nation or *discrimination* in conjunction with the word *racism*. And something else they did. They usually, or often, made no distinction between beliefs and attitudes or beliefs and social practices. Prejudice, as psychologists or social psychologists said in their books, as social psychologist Gordon Allport said in his seminal study of the phenomenon, *The Nature of Prejudice*,[1] involved attitudes, prejudgmental attitudes, that could be applied to anything—not just to race, but to religion, or to politics—almost anything. Thus, prejudice did not have to involve race at all, and yet in America, the two words were interchangeable, as if they were the same thing. If prejudice denoted prejudgmental attitudes, then beliefs were something different, because beliefs were different from attitudes. In the literature one could see the phrase *prejudicial beliefs*, but the beliefs might not be explained, or they would be explained in a way that was not clear. White supremacy was one of those beliefs, and it was very unclear the way one usually saw it in the literature. It was unclear in Du Bois's writings. Like others, Du Bois used white supremacy to refer to "prejudicial beliefs" that white people had toward black people or Black people. But white supremacist beliefs were, logically, beliefs, "prejudicial beliefs," about white people, that is, beliefs that white people concocted and applied to themselves in a prejudgmental manner. Prejudicial beliefs toward Black people would have to be of another kind, would have to have another name. Du Bois, as well as others writing on racism, knew there were prejudicial beliefs for Black people and talked about them but had no name for them, except names that were unclear, or unenlightening, such as *white supremacy*, which really applied to white people, and *caste*, or *color caste*, as Du Bois would use, or *racial caste*, which Du Bois and others would use, which did not make a distinction always, or even often, among belief, attitude, social condition, or social practice.

And then there was the word *racism*. It came into the literature on race, racial prejudice, and prejudicial beliefs roughly after the Second World War. The Nazis' experience brought this word into use and, with it, confusion. The Nazis, as racists, had been racist against Jews, in particular, but also against slavic and black people, homosexuals, and gypsies. The Jews had been white, the Slavs had been white, and black people had been black. Yet the Nazis treated them all in a racist fashion. This meant that racism cut across race. But the literature did not significantly pick up on this larger understanding, because the word *racism* immediately became used interchangeably with the word *race*, and phrases like *race prejudice, racial beliefs,* or *racial discrimination,* which could be seen rendered in the literature as *racist discrimination.* Another way of saying what had occurred is that the word *racism* not only became associated almost exclusively with race, but specifically with the white race and the black race in America, with white people being the racists and black or Black people being the victims. The more expansive view of racism was not seen, or not seen clearly by people and, effectively, lost.

I did not see its expansive significance for years. It only showed how, when ideas, beliefs, or social behavior get locked into history, they become resistant to change. It also showed how history, that is, how human beings engaging in behavior in time and over time, co-opted new words, ideas, beliefs, or social practices and subsumed them under old labels or understandings to conserve or preserve the traditional, old orientations or realities. Human beings have investments, or stakes, in the things that they believe in, know best, or which matter to them the most, the things that augment their lives, or things that they do in their lives, or things that detract from or diminish both realities. In Black America, the understanding of race and negative racial practices against Blacks was related directly to the question of leadership and its appropriateness or legitimacy, to the power of individuals or groups, to various kinds of monetary rewards—governmental grants, salaries, donations, or scholarships—or to ameliorative, corrective, or progressive social programs, public or private. The word *racism*, when it came into use, was not associated with any of these things. It came from another place, associated with other things. But when Blacks took on that word, they quickly associated it with race, and all the things that race stood for or that were associated with race in Black life, from leadership legitimacy to corrective, liberating social programs. It is doubtful that this co-opting was done consciously or even selfishly. It occurred primarily because of a traditional understanding and a long-standing historical practice of thinking and acting on race, which meant that it mainly occurred in an unconscious fashion among Blacks.

But the effect of it all was to obscure and suppress the meaning and reality of racism. It all obscured and suppressed the understanding for me until I began reading Du Bois a lot closer. Some of his later writings, in the traditional jargon of *race* or *race prejudice*, could be seen to have to do with more than race. Then, going back over the earlier writings, I could see that he always wrote about more than race when he wrote on that subject. What effected the transition in my thinking was a comment that Du Bois made in 1944, in an article he wrote entitled "Prospect of a World Without Racial Conflict." He did not mention in the article (although in newspaper columns years before, as I discovered in my research on him) the trip he had made to Nazi Germany in 1936. He had gone there with others to study the German educational system. He stayed in the country six months, not only observing the educational system but also German life under Adolf Hitler and the Nazi regime, which induced Du Bois to say that Germany was a land of "whispers." He observed the lives of Jews in Germany and the way the Nazis and other Germans treated the Jews. He had seen German-Jewish relations before, in the 1890s, when he was a student at the University of Berlin. He used the phrase anti-Semitism to describe the German beliefs, attitudes, and practices toward the Jews in Germany. He had observed the same thing in the United States before he went to Germany to study and when he returned home. But in Germany, in 1936, he knew and said that the punitive treatment of Jews was more verbose, violent, and suppressive than it had been in the early 1890s. In the article of 1944, he consciously and explicitly indicated an understanding that his discussions of race went beyond race and that he always knew that when he used phrases like *race, race prejudice, racial prejudice, color caste,* or *racial discrimination,* he was talking about more than race. In his article he wrote, not using the phrase anti-Semitism, but "race hate": "Of course, many of the usual characteristics were missing in this outbreak of race hate in Germany. There was in reality little physical difference between German and Jew. . . . Nevertheless, the ideological basis of this attack was that of fundamental biological difference showing itself in spiritual and cultural incompatibility."[2]

Here was Du Bois saying clearly that the Germans and the Jews were of the same white race, but that the Germans were persecuting them anyway. He also said something else implicitly momentous, that the Germans created in their own minds (by an ideology) an abstract, fanciful, mystical, and nonexistent racial status for Jews, or "race" for the Jews. This "race" was pure fabrication and was composed of abstract, fanciful, mystical, and nonexistent attributes that determined the thought and social behavior of that "race." The Germans, then, imposed this abstract, fanciful, nonexistent "race" on the Jewish people and believed that the abstract, fanciful, and mystical constructions were actual in-born traits of the Jews. And the Germans related to these fancifully constructed traits not only as if they were the actual innate or natural attributes of Jews, but as if they were "innate" traits that determined their thoughts and social behavior and which the Germans felt they had to punish.

In 1953, after visiting the Jewish ghetto in Warsaw, Du Bois said the following in a speech: "No, the race problem in which I was interested cut across lines of color and physique and belief and status and was a matter of cultural patterns, perverted teaching and human hate and prejudice, which reached all sorts of people and caused endless evil to all men."[3]

In these comments, Du Bois was saying something as profound as in the previous comments. He said that the "race problem" cut across race. But he said more than that, that this problem cut across "belief and status" and reached and affected "all sorts of people," a reference to ethnic groups, social classes, or gender groups. Du Bois was saying that racists could treat anybody, any collectivity of people and its individuals in a racist fashion. All they had to do was to devise some racist beliefs about any of the collectivities that created an abstract, fanciful, mystical, and nonexistent "race," with "nonexistent" attributes and then impose this "race" and its nonexistent attributes on an actual human collectivity and its individual members and then relate to the collectivity and the individuals in it as if these were their real attributes and then penalize them for having them.

Indeed, it could be said that Du Bois had an understanding that race and racial prejudice went beyond race as early as the 1880s. In his autobiographies, he recalled how the Irish were treated by other white people in his village of Great Barrington, as if they were innately inferior people. In the early 1890s in Germany, as a student, he noted that the Jews were treated by other Germans in ways similar to the ways the Irish were treated in his village and the way Black people were treated elsewhere in the United States. Du Bois also knew that women generally were victims of a similar kind of behavior and also believed that lower-class people could suffer the same fate. In a 1912 speech he said, "if democracy tries to exclude women or Negroes or the poor or any class because of innate characteristics."[4] All kinds of people, and as Du Bois knew and understood, could be treated in what he called a racial or racially prejudiced manner. He knew this early on. But after eighty years of writing on race or racial prejudice and overwhelmingly focusing on white people and Black people and White race prejudice toward Blacks, Du Bois did not always remember how flexibly and profoundly he understood this phenomenon. What he understood was racism without the concept. But when he took it on later in life, he still did not employ it separately from his concept of race or race prejudice and similar concepts; he used the new term interchangeably with them. But had Du Bois discussed race prejudice in the complex, profound way he understood it, had he tried to convince Black or white people of it, he probably would have had no, or very few takers. He would have run up against the entrenched, traditional view. People, Black people especially, but also white people, would not have understood his views and would have ignored them or criticized them or rejected them. Editors of journals or publishing companies would have had difficulty with his views and would probably have rejected them in an example of historical process that could have lost Du Bois to us. The idea that race, racial beliefs, or race prejudice were the accurate and profound realities that they were was centuries old, in Europe, in America, and in other parts of the world.

The understandings of race and race prejudice made their appearance in Western history and civilization during what historians call Middle Ages in Europe. They grew out of the relationship between white people and black Africans and black Arabs, or Moors, in Western Europe. But it wasn't until about the sixteenth century that the idea that race and races were superior and inferior and the mephitic prejudice against race and, namely, the black race, seriously began in Western Europe. It grew out of white Western Europeans engaging in an African slave trade and grossly exploiting black African slave labor in the Western Hemisphere. It was also affected by Whites/Europeans who exterminated Indians and took their land, putting African slave labor on it to work it.

What white Europeans were doing was totally against their beliefs, the lofty, universal ideals, values, and morality that they considered defining of themselves and their civilization; against the universal humanistic thought that they developed for their civilization, which they touted, which they felt elevated them above other people in the world. But the Europeans had no intention of stopping their malevolent behavior. The African slave trade, the use of African slave labor, and the exploitation of land and mineral wealth that formerly belonged to the Indians gave vast wealth to Europeans, which they used to develop Europe on an accelerated basis. It would take European civilization beyond other civilizations of the time: in technology, science, commerce, governmental efficiency, military capablity, and other ways.

In the sixteenth century a huge gap opened up between what Europeans believed and professed and the way they behaved. They had their lofty, even humane Christian, liberal, and emerging democratic ideals, as well as a number of other philosophies that stressed human dignity, human decency, and human morality. In their behavior they contradicted and violated every one of these lofty universal ideals and their exalted universal morality. The Europeans in these days knew they were wrong in what they were doing. Their lofty, universal idealities and humane sentiments told them that they were and indicted them for what they were doing, a part of which was their refusal to implement their professed universal idealities and their perversion of them. But they cast aside the indictment and condemnation and consciously did wrong anyway. What they did consciously and intentionally was to conduct holocausts against Indians and Africans that would last for centuries.

Du Bois captured the African Holocaust in his book *The Negro*, published in 1915:

> These were not days of decadence, but a period that gave the world Shakespeare, Martin Luther, and Raphael, Haroun-al-Raschid and Abraham Lincoln. It was the day of the greatest expansion of two of the world's most pretentious religions and of the beginnings of the modern organization of industry. In the midst of this advance and uplift this slave trade and this slavery spread more human misery, inculcated more disrespect for and neglect of humanity, a greater callousness to suffering, and more petty, cruel, human hatred than can well be calculated. We may excuse and palliate it, and write history so as to let men forget it; it remains the most inexcusable and despicable blot on modern human history.[5]

What the Whites/Europeans did to Africans and Indians represented the greatest destruction of human life and cultures and the grossest exploitation of labor, land, and raw materials the world had ever seen. The behavior lasted for centuries and included the hatred, inhumanity, and cruelty that Whites/Europeans exhibited and carried out against people to achieve outcomes that benefitted Whites/Europeans and European civilization and its development. Those white Western intellectuals today who criticize earlier European/Western efforts to spread their assumed universal ideals, saying now that it was oppressive and destructive of peoples, cultures, and human differences, indulge in a false criticism. What they have yet to understand is that Whites/Europeans made little to no effort to spread genuine universal humanistic or genuine universal ideals of liberty, equality, or freedom among the world's populations. They spread and implemented perverted universal humanistic ideals, the word, but not the truth, morality, and spirituality of freedom, and this contributed to the destruction of peoples, cultures, and countries and to their colonization, suppression, and exploitation.

And the Whites/Europeans found a way to keep the horrors of their behavior, the violation and severe perversion of their lofty universal idealities and morality and the destruction they wrought from their own perceptions and understanding. A way to keep the contradictions of their loftiness and lowliness from totally ravaging or exploding their personalities and desiccating their civilization was to devise strands of racist beliefs that produced ameliorative racist protection, such as racist thinking, racist social behavior, and racist psychologies that all functioned to deprecate the humanity and human status of other people to facilitate and justify moving against them. Whites/Europeans devised three initial kinds of racist beliefs for ameliorative protection and mephitic purposes: white supremacy, redicism, and ebonicism.

In my research on racism, when I began to understand what it really was and how many forms it could actually take, I saw that there were no names for some of these forms, and that names which existed were inaccurately understood and used. In 1987, I published an article called "The Faces of Racism,"[6] putting in print understandings and descriptions of different kinds of racist beliefs and racist realities that I had been working with for some time. These racist beliefs were distinctive, even though similar; this is also true about the different forms of racism. In the article I referred to seven different clusters of racist beliefs and, thus, of seven different forms of racism, inventing some names for some beliefs and forms. I referred to *white supremacy*, racist beliefs and practices that applied to white people; *ebonicism*, racist beliefs and practices that applied to black and Black people; *redicism*, racist beliefs and practices against Indians; *xanthicism*, racist beliefs and practices against yellow people, or Asians; *anti-Jewism* (instead of anti-Semitism, for Arabs are also Semites), racist beliefs and practices against Jews; *bronzism,* racist beliefs and practices against bronze-skin Hispanic people; and *sexism,* racist beliefs and practices against women. After publication of my article, I devised another racist conceptualization, *maleism,* which was racist beliefs and practices that men engaged in toward themselves to refer to their alleged natural superiority.

An important thing to note about racist beliefs is that they are always implemented in a paired manner. When racists relate to their victims, they do so on the basis of beliefs that allege their own innate or natural superiority and on the basis of racist beliefs that allege the innate or natural inferiority of their victims. It may be that both sets of racist beliefs are not articulated, either orally or in writing, but the one not articulated is always there. It is always there as conscious thought, unconcious thought, as attitude, as feeling, and as physiological manifestations such as hate-filled eyes, malignant facial expressions, heightened adrenalin, or physical gestures. In America, white supremacy and ebonicism have always been joined together and, thus, have always been white supremacy/ebonicism. Also always paired in America have been white supremacy/redicism, white supremacy/xanthicism, and maleism/sexism.

The Whites/Europeans developed white supremacist, redicist, and ebonicistic racist beliefs and practices to legitimize killing Indians and taking their lands in the Western Hemisphere and to transport black Africans to the region to work the land and to exploit their labor. These beliefs and practices were also employed in an intellectual and psychological manner to rationalize and justify gross and inhumane behavior toward Indians and black Africans to keep the brains and insides of Whites/Europeans from wrenching or exploding and to keep their lofty beliefs and ideals from being rendered meaningless to them. This rationalization and justification had to be very strong in terms of content, in terms of cultural and social embediment, and in terms of conscious and unconscious internalization, because Whites/Europeans engaged in this kind of gross inhumane behavior (according to their own lofty standards) for centuries. They not only had to convince themselves that they were not wrong in what they were doing, but that they were engaged in righteous and moral behavior, and even acting in a beneficient and progressive manner in history.

Racist beliefs and racist practices, as the history of these occurrences—as European and American racist history both show—cut across race, involving different races of people as victims. But these beliefs and practices, upon finite analysis, which I was finally able to make, went not only beyond race, but even beyond human status and humanity. If actual people such as Indians or Africans could be viewed as being nonhumans or subhumans, this functioning of racism would make it possible to keep Western culture and civilization from being totally damaged psychically, morally, and spiritually, especially if humanistic or human liberation thought and behavior could be implemented in the culture and civilization among Whites to some extent. But great psychical, moral, and spiritual damage would still be done to culture and civilization and to the people of those realities, who participated in them, were vested by them, and perpetuated them.

But this evidence of racist functioning and racist damage in Europe and America and in other places in the Western Hemisphere, was obscured from the people who were the racists and who practiced racism. Obscured from view for centuries was the fact that race and the concepts that grew from it, such as racial beliefs, racial thinking, racial prejudice, and the racial practices that grew out of this believing and thinking, were predicated on racist beliefs, racist assumptions, and racist practices. An inadequate and even false understanding of a miasmic and devastating social phenomenon was perpetuated for centuries by learned as well as average human beings.

The British and then white Americans did the most in Western civilization to emphasize race, and, thus, to obscure and suppress racism from the view and consciousness of people. The British came to America in the seventeenth century with strong, dichotomous views about the color white and the color black, the principal color scheme and color symbolization in their language, culture, and social life. White to the British meant moral, good, benevolent, worthy, beautiful, innocent, chaste, clean, unblemished, and the like. Black meant to them immoral, evil, sinful, sinister, corrupt, treacherous, dangerous, guilty, ugly, melancholy, dirty, soiled, and so on. The British planted their white-black color scheme and white-black color symbolization and meaning in their colonies in North America. The red or reddish-brown color of the Indians contrasted with the British primary color scheme and color symbolization, but it caused only momentary hesitation and confusion. The British wanted the land of the Indians, which they took, rationalizing and justifying by what I call their redicist beliefs and practices against the Indians. These beliefs were obscured by their racial focus, that is, their redicist predicated racial beliefs and practices.

The British did not set up a hierarchical racial-social relationship with the Indians when they established their colonies in North America and pushed the Indians out of them or confined them to a section or sections. Except for some individual Indians, the British did not want them in their daily lives. British extermination and reservationizing practices accounted for this exclusion.

The British established a white race over black race hierarchical racial-social relationship in their colonies in North America. They brought Africans to the colonies as slaves who, of necessity, would interact with the British and other Europeans who settled in the British colonies on a daily basis. The British augmented and sealed this hierarchical racial-social relationship by their white-black color scheme and color symbolization, to which other Europeans in the colonies adhered and promoted, joining with the British in locking these ideational attributes tightly into the culture and social life of the colonies and in the minds and personalities of the white people who dominated the colonies and the black people in them, first the black Africans, and then the Black people, a new ethnic group of the black race that evolved from their African slave forebears. The racist-inundated white race over black race hierarchical racial-social relationship passed into the new American history and the construction of the new American nation-state. As in the British colonies, it was anchored and locked in place by white people being masters and black people or Black people being slaves or nonslaves, who were often treated as if they were slaves. The white-black color scheme and color symbolization contributed to the locking and anchoring. Other things did as well, such as White political power, slave laws, racist laws, White cruelty, White violence, and numerous White legal and social proscriptions against Blacks, slave and nonslave.

The white British and white Americans were both obsessed with color and race, the white color and the white race and the black color and the black race. This helped to obscure from their own consciousness, thinking, and perceptions, their other obsession, which was not race, but "race." This meant that the white supremacist racist doctrine that they had developed for themselves in order to interact with Indians, which they also employed when interacting with black Africans and then all Black people, was never seen as a racist doctrine, but only as a racial doctrine, which in their minds was only about

race. The cluster of racist beliefs that they developed about Indians
and black Africans and then all Black people, both in the colonies
and then in America, which I have called redicist and ebonicistic racist
beliefs, were understood only as racial beliefs and pertained only to
races, namely, to the red and black race.

The British and white Americans were extreme in what they understood as their racial thinking with respect to Blacks. They wanted
the latter only to think of themselves through their color and race.
They did not want their Black slaves, or even nonslave Blacks, to think
that they had a beginning outside slavery or, as in the case of nonslave
Blacks outside subordination. They did not want Blacks, slaves or
nonslaves, to think that they came from some other part of the world,
that they had had their own histories, their own cultures, and own
identities, based on their histories and cultures, prior to coming to
North America. They wanted Black people, slaves and nonslaves, to
think of themselves as being historyless, cultureless, and as having
only a color or racial identity. Another identity, a slave identity, was
also emphasized, but that identity also had to carry the word *black*
with it, and thus a dual identity of black and slave was created, but
understood to be one single identity, with *black* and *slave* used interchangeably. White people made race the overwhelming thought
line, the overwhelming understanding, the overwhelming perception,
the overwhelming symbolization, the overwhelming social reality, and
the overwhelming survival and developmental reality in America.
White people did not want to escape from race and did not want
Black people to escape from it, that is, the White view that the white
race was superior and the black race was inferior.

But all the years—these centuries—that white people emphasized
race and rammed it down the throats of Blacks (and also down their
own throats), Blacks always knew that white people related to them
in ways that went beyond race. Black people had no problem being
identified in racial terms, recognizing and accepting their varied dark-
ness in color but also other similar and varied biological features.
They saw how they physically contrasted with white people, who also,
as they saw, had varied white skin color and other general and varied
biological features. Blacks understood as Whites understood that it
was the contrasting biological attributes between them (and not the
similar biological features between them) that divided them into separate races. But race, referring to white or black people, was a reference to human status and to humanity or to put it another way, to

Other. But Black people, slave and nonslave, throughout their history in America always knew that white people were trying to and did treat them as if they were not human beings or full human beings—or, and to use peculiar language again, as *Non-Others*: as something other than human beings and belonging to something other than the human race. What Blacks, slaves and nonslaves, perceived were beliefs, thoughts, understandings, and perceptions that existed behind White racial projections in these areas, behind White racial practices. If Black slave and nonslave Blacks had had the word or concept of racism and had been able to counter the concept of race and break through racial talk, they would have been able to tell themselves and white people what white people were promoting, and the way Whites really victimized them in the United States.

Actually, it was white people who made the disclosure public, although they did not understand it, because they used the word *race* and explained it in racial terms. Blacks could not counter what Whites were doing or explain to them what they were doing in a counter argument because they had only the concept of race, and things like racial beliefs, racial thinking, and race prejudice to work with. But in the nineteenth century, white people made it clear, even if they did not make it clear to themselves, that they were espousing racist beliefs and not racial beliefs, because their public and private talk in that century, was not about human status and humanity, the human status and the humanity of Blacks, but their nonhumanity or subhumanity. White people in the nineteenth century publicly and privately referred to Black people as animals or creatures, which in their minds and beliefs took Blacks outside a human status. In the nineteenth century, white people in America and in Europe finally said plainly what they had always thought and felt about black people or Black people and what had been the basis of their treatment of them.

The noted American scientist Louis Agassiz was no longer willing to bite his tongue. In a writing of the nineteenth century, prior to the mid-nineteenth-century war, he said that the brain of black people bore a strong resemblance "in several particulars to the brain of an ourangoutang."[7] Later in the century, two individuals wrote in a science magazine the following about black people, with Blacks in the United States being the primary target of their remarks: "When all inhibitions of a high order have been removed by sexual excitement, I fail to see any difference from a physical standpoint between the sexual furor of the negro and that which prevails among the lower animals in certain instances and at certain periods . . . namely, that *furor sexualis* in the negro resembles similar sexual attacks in the bull and elephant."[8]

In Europe in 1830 the renowned German philosopher, Georg Hegel, said about black people, "The Negro represents natural man in all his wild and untamed nature. If you want to treat and understand him rightly, you must abstract all elements of respect and morality and sensitivity—there is nothing remotely humanized in the Negro character."[9]

Hegel did not say directly that black people were animals, but when he stripped them of their humanity by his remarks and talked of them being "wild and untamed," it was clear what he thought them to be. Later in the nineteenth century, the French intellectual Georges Courier wrote: "The Negro race . . . is marked by black complexion, crisped or woolly hair, compressed cranium and a flat nose. The projection of the lower parts of the face, and the thick lips, evidently approximate it to the monkey tribe; the hordes of which it consists have always remained in the most complete state of barbarism."[10] The British explorer and writer Richard Burton wrote, "The study of the negro is the study of man's rudimentary mind. He would appear rather a degeneracy from the civilized man than a savage rising to the first step, were it not for his total incapacity for improvement."[11]

As the quotations show, white people in America and Europe in the nineteenth century were racists. They engaged in racial thinking, but it only obscured who they really were and the kind of thinking in which they really engaged. They had to start with race because there were the obvious white race and the obvious black race, and white people had for centuries made race the focus. For centuries, white people made race matter. But over that lengthy period of time, race mattered only in a secondary manner. What really mattered was racism. That meant that what really mattered to white people not only in the nineteenth century, but in centuries before, was "race" and "races"—the white "race," the black "race," and the red "race." These were not actual races, except this actuality in a secondary manner. The main concern was with invisible, nonexistent "races," with an invisible, nonexistent white "race" that had fanciful, abstract, mystical, nonexistent alleged attributes that were of a superior quality and to be praised and glorified and an invisible, nonexistent black "race" and Indian or red "race" that had fanciful, abstract, mystical, non-

existent alleged attributes of an inferior quality that were to be condemned, and for which Indian and black people were to be punished.

But more than that, in the minds of white people, the attributes
of the white "race," which white people regarded as being true or
actual representations of themselves, added up to the white "race"
being a "race" of gods or godlike entities. Also in their minds, the
black "race" and red "race" constituted "races" of nonhumans or
subhumans. In America, white people have historically, that is continuously, related to themselves as if they were godly or godlike, and
to Blacks and Indians as if they were nonhuman or subhuman; as
Non-Others. Du Bois understood this all the years he spoke and
wrote about race or race prejudice, or racial discrimination. But the
latter conceptual paraphernalia prevented him from speaking more
clearly on the matter. It prevented others, too, from expressing in-
sights in a full and more enlightening way.

When people are perceived to be nonhuman or subhuman, this
takes things beyond simple prejudice, or bigotry, or discrimination.
When people are perceived this way, they are perceived to be outside
a human status, outside humanity, and outside human morality, and
therefore, outside having human rights. If they are not human beings
and do not have human rights, then there is no way they are entitled
to have political or civil rights. And since being nonhuman or subhuman is forever, then such people would always be denied political
and civil rights, and even simple human dignity, decency, and cour-
tesy—if the racists had their way.

To put it succinctly and as the history of white people, Black people, Indians, and American history shows: racists are *anti–human being* and *anti-humanity*. Anybody who thinks like this will be
prejudiced, bigoted, and discriminatory. But none of these words describe a racist and what a racist is or does. Racists put actual human
beings, including themselves, outside the boundaries of morality, so
that they can relate to actual people, their victims, in a nonmoral
manner; where they can relate to these people any way they wish,
violently, abusively, discriminatorily, and without any pangs of conscience or guilt. No matter what they did to their victims, they would
be guiltless, innocent, and nonresponsible. These kinds of responses
or feelings pertained to human beings and interacting with human
beings. They did not pertain to nonhumans or subhumans.

There is a theme in American historical and literary writing, such
as novels, plays, and poetry, but which can also be seen in television

programs and movies and which is the theme of *innocence*, often referred to as *American innocence*. This reference, of course, is not really to America, which is innocent, but to white racists, and White racist America, which are not. How could they be? Not after the way white racists have treated Black people and other people of color in this country. But when a people look upon themselves as being gods or godlike and other people as being nonhuman or subhuman, they can think this way. Gods or godlike people can't do wrong, and no wrong can be done to nonhumans or subhumans. In that nexus pops out White innocence in America, which is strictly fanciful, delusional, and a denial of reality—manifestations of the way racism has affected the thinking, psychology, morality, and spirituality of white people. There are white male historians and political scientists especially, who talk of Americans, meaning white Americans, "losing their innocence," commencing with their involvement in the First World War. This loss continued in the twentieth century as a consequence of participating in more wars and becoming a global (i.e., a colonial imperialistic) power. This position either accepts the extermination and reservationizing of Indians, the enslavement and segregation of Blacks, and the denial of rights, equality, and opportunities to Indians, Blacks, and even white women, as acts of innocence, of nonsuppression or noncruelty, of no importance or significance, or as acts that in no way reflect pathological thinking, pathological psychological attributes, and pathological social behavior among the perpetrators of the behavior.

A continuing inadequacy among Black intellectuals, Black leaders, and other Blacks is that they do not really or significantly deal with racism. They are locked into race and its accompanying conceptual paraphernalia. Talk about race in America is invariably talk about Black people, not about white people. It is invariably talk about how racism has affected Black people, but not about how it has affected white people, which is critical to how it has affected Black people; for it is white people as victims of their own racism and racist afflictions that account for the insidious ways that they relate to Blacks, doing damage to them. And these same racist afflictions tell white people that they do not do any damage to themselves or to Black people, and that Blacks do this to themselves. White people see themselves as being guiltless, innocent, and nonresponsible. In a recent book, *Race Matters*,[12] Cornel West discusses race and how it mattered. But he, like other Black intellectuals, or other Blacks who focus on race, did not see how it mattered secondarily. West cracked on Black people for their racial thinking and other inadequacies. He made no reference to any white inadequacies, and in not doing so, conveyed the impression that they did not exist. His whole discussion of race, which essentially excluded white people from the blighted situation of Blacks, confirmed for white readers of his book, that they and other Whites in America were guiltless, innocent, and nonresponsible. And West did more than that. Like white racists, he blamed most Black people for their own depressed situation in America, claiming that their development of a nihilistic disposition, which reflected depression, hopelessness, self-hatred, and the lack of self-love, dislocated and enervated them and prevented them from dealing effectively with their blighted situation. Whites were in no way, or in no significant way, associated with this supposed nihilism and its debilitating, enervating effects. Presumably these defects were to be found among Blacks themselves, in their minds, personalities, or social behavior, or in the cultural-social environment of Blacks that invested these things in their minds, psychology, and social behavior. In either case with Blacks or their environment, in West's view, it was a matter of deep-seated and widespread pathology—and pathology, in both cases, not associated or associated significantly with white people and their intellectual, psychological, moral, and spiritual afflictions, or their miasmic behavior toward Blacks.

While other Black intellectuals and other articulate Blacks do not subscribe to a Black nihilism, they, like West, say very little about the effects of racism on white people or about White racist behavior toward Blacks, and therefore, like West, blame most Black people for their depressed situation in America and essentially exonerate white people from any sigificant involvement. This means that Black intellectuals and other Blacks who discuss race and not racism or associate racism exclusively with race, ironically abet White racism in America—ideals, beliefs, values, and social practices—and help to promote it. Their discussion has to be on racism, and that means that their discussion has extensively to be on white people, in terms of how racism has afflicted and continues to afflict them and how their racism has affected American history, culture, and social life, and also Blacks in America. Racism matters in America, but it mainly matters as an ideal and practice, to white people and White racist America. This is an urgent understanding that white, black, and other people in America need, and it is the urgent basis on which this book will continue to proceed.

3.

White and Black Alienation in America

Alienation is a provocative subject, and it has therefore had various kinds of interpretations. Another reason for the various viewpoints is that people from different academic disciplines, such as history, philosophy, psychology, and social psychology have taken a crack at it and have tried to describe it and define it. Poets, fiction writers, playwrights, and artists have also taken their turns at it as have also television and movie script writers and television and movie directors. The following descriptions have come from these various sources. Alienation means being disenchanted, dispirited, hostile to, separated from, not belonging to, not being fulfilled while belonging, being involved but feeling detached or uncommitted, being a part of but feeling resentment. And the sources talk about a wide range of psychological dispositions that could be found in any form of alienation: fear, anxiety, anger, depression, insecurity, cynicism, or belligerence. Alienation is an exciting dimension of human existence and an exciting thing to study.

My first formal encounter with alienation came from my study of Russian history. It was a concept that historians used in association with a group in that history known as the intelligentsia. The latter was not a reference to intellectuals. Russia had intellectuals, as did other countries of Europe, as did America and other countries. The Russian intelligentsia were something else. Among them might be individuals with great intellectual ability, but others who would not be engaged in any significant intellectual activity at all, not in writing or even significant discussion, and who might even be rather intolerant of either activity. The Russian Christian Existentialist philosopher Nicholas Berdyaev described the Russian intelligentsia best. He said they constituted a subculture in Russia that was predicated on and held together by ideas, particularly social ideas, to which members had to adhere and be loyal and which they had to try to implement in Russian society.

The Russian intelligentsia were created by the Russian tsars, but not intentionally. Between Peter the Great in the eighteenth century and Nicholas II in the early twentieth century, Russia underwent modernization. It was done mainly by borrowing from Western European countries: military, technology, political and educational institutions, financial techniques, languages, architecture, art, philosophical thought and other things. With Peter the Great and other tsars of the eighteenth century, members of the Russian nobility were sent abroad to study in Western European universities or institutes, to acquire knowledge and skills, and familiarity with Western culture, so that they could help implement the culture in Russia upon their return to the country to help modernize it.

But some of what the Russian nobility or their children learned abroad, such as certain political, philosophical, or social ideas, made them critical of Russia upon their return home, of its strong, even oppressive state, of serfdom, of censorship, of restrictions on public assembly, or on physical movements. The Russian tsars also exposed themselves to criticism from another angle. Their efforts to Westernize or modernize Russia mainly benefitted them, their power, wealth, and political reach, the Russian state, and the Russian nobility. The latter, indeed, became more Western oriented, especially German or French, and less Russian. Modernization that Westernized Russia, however, opened up a huge cultural gap between the Russian nobility and the mass of the people, who were serfs and peasants. Throughout most of the period between Peter the Great and Nicholas I, the Russian tsars refused to build a middle class in their country, afraid of the political and economic demands it would make. A middle class would have closed the cultural gap. It would have been an assimilator and beneficiary of Westernization and would have been the means, by example or by working with or through the state as members of it, to spread Westernization and modernization downward in Russian society.

But the Russian tsars, until Alexander II in the mid- and late nineteenth century, refused to build a middle class and also made no significant effort to push Westernization and modernization to the bottom of Russian society to close the cultural gap. This brought on public criticism, initially, and for the longest time from individuals from the Russian nobility. They not only criticized the tsars and the state, but also the Russian nobility for being what they called, in reference to their very privileged position, superfluous people. These critical individuals of the aristocracy became alienated from their own class and also alienated from the Russian tsars and Russian state and even from Russian society. By the early nineteenth century, such individuals were numerous enough to form a subculture in Russia, which was itself alienated from Russian society as it was. The intelligentsia subculture wanted changes and proposed changes, but they were usually kept out of the state and other institutions that could have been used to implement changes. This deprived the Russian intelligentsia of experience in using the state and other institutions to design and implement practical cultural and social changes in Russia. This left them only with their ideas or their dreams, which they clung to, as well as with a wide range of psychological responses that reinforced their clinging to ideas and dreams, such as impatience, anxiety, hatred, cynicism, intolerance, or belligerence, which became rooted in the subculture and which were invested in those who joined it and functioned from it. In the latter nineteenth and early twentieth centuries, individuals from other classes joined the intelligentsia, making it a subculture of mixed social ranks, or *raznochintsy*. In the later nineteenth century, revolutionaries appeared in the intelligentsia subculture who imbibed Karl Marx's thinking. The Bolsheviks became part of the subculture in the early twentieth century and would, changing their name to communists in 1918, take over Russia and with the aid of masses of people build the Soviet Union.

When I began studying Black history and American history and the interaction between the two, I saw similarities between these two histories and Russian history. America had slavery, and for most serfs that was what Russia's serfdom really was. The Russian tsars, the Russian state, and the Russian nobility refused for centuries to end serfdom in the country. In America presidents, Congresses, state

governments, and the rich and powerful of the country in the North
and, of course, in the South refused to end slavery and, like forces in
Russia, did things to entrench servitude, including suppressing forces
that sought abolition. In Russia, an intelligentsia emerged to be a
critical, moral voice in the country, to attack serfdom, and other aspects of Russian society. In the early nineteenth century in America,
Black intellectuals emerged as a group, and they became a critical,
moral voice, one that attacked racism, slavery, and efforts to colonize
(or to deport) nonslave Blacks from the country, as well as the politics
and immorality of the country. Black intellectuals had some of the
characteristics of the Russian intelligentsia. There were individuals
with intellectual capabilities among them, as well as individuals that
were more activist than intellectual. The ranks of Black intellectuals
were also "mixed," with Black middle-class elements and former
slaves in the group. There was also a mixture of religious and secular
elements. Black intellectuals, like the Russian intelligentsia, were held
together by social ideas, especially the idea of ending servitude; also
like the Russian intelligentsia they had divisions among themselves,
based on ideas and tenacious clinging to them. Black intellectuals
were also considerably kept out of political institutions and were thus
not able to use them to promote cultural or social change. Black
intellectuals were also alienated like the Russian intelligentsia, but not
from American society; they were alienated from the White racism of
American society, from White racist America.

Du Bois captured the historical alienation of Black intellectuals and
Black people in general in America; as well as the historical alienation
of white people in the country, in comments he made in *The Souls of
Black Folk* in 1903. They constitute a good framework through which
to analyze these historical forms of alienation in America. In his most
influential single writing, Du Bois remarked:

> The Negro is a sort of seventh son, born with a veil, and
> gifted with a second-sight in this American world,—a
> world which yields him no true self-consciousness, but only
> lets him see himself through the revelation of the other
> world. It is a peculiar sensation, this double-consciousness,
> this sense of always looking at one's self through the eyes
> of others, of measuring one's soul by the tape of a world
> that looks on in amused contempt and pity. One ever feels
> his twoness,—an American, a Negro; two souls, two

thoughts, two unreconciled strivings; two warring ideals in one dark body, whose dogged strength alone keeps it from being torn asunder.[1]

Du Bois also proposed a solution to the problem of the alienation of Black people in other comments that he made:

> The history of the American Negro is the history of this strife,—this longing to attain self-conscious manhood, to merge this double self into a better and truer self. In this merging he wishes neither of the older selves to be lost. He would not Africanize America, for America has too much to teach the world and Africa. He would not bleach his Negro soul in a flood of white Americanism, for he knows that Negro blood has a message for the world. He simply wishes to make it possible for a man to be both a Negro and an American, without being cursed and spit upon by his fellows, without having the doors of Opportunity closed roughly in his face.[2]

Du Bois's remarks have captured the interest of many Black intellectuals or other articulate Black people since the time they were penned. But in my view, most intellectual reactions to Du Bois's comments have been superficial and wanting. And there is a reason for this. Most Black intellectuals do not know much about Du Bois's thought. People will drop his name, verbalize homage to him, and quote him but otherwise will show little to no evidence that they have read and studied his vast corpus of thought. In his book *Prophetic Fragments* Cornel West said of Du Bois that he was not a "major theoretical thinker." His full comments were: "It is no accident that the disproportionate number of black socialist intellectuals in the USA since WW II have yet to produce a major Black socialist theorist (I consider neither Du Bois nor Oliver Cox major theoretical thinkers)."[3] As I have said, I wrote a dissertation on Du Bois's socialist analysis, which was nearly five hundred pages in typescript. I have a draft volume of Du Bois's prescriptive socialist theories, including his theory of history, which I will complete writing one of these days. I also have a draft of his philosophy of scientific sociology (social science), which I will also complete one of these times. I know of a scholar who has completed a study of Du Bois's theory of consciousness. One could write a substantial volume on Du Bois's theory of racism.

Du Bois had something in common with Karl Marx. Marx did not write theoretical treatises. His various theories, of history, society, social praxis, revolution, morality, alienation, or labor are found dispersed throughout his writings. What Marx did was to make theoretical comments in his writings, sometimes of an extended nature. But to know any of Marx's theories in full, it would be necessary to go through his writings and pull out all the theoretical comments he made in each theoretical area. Now, Karl Marx did not do this. A vast number of intellectuals who proclaim themselves disciples did this.

Du Bois has not had this kind of thing happen to him and his thought. He wrote for eighty years, and his corpus of thought is waiting for theoretical disclosure in numerous areas. There is a difficulty in studying Du Bois's thought because he often understated things. He also did not provide much conceptionalization in his writings. You had to know certain subjects by name or conceptualization before reading Du Bois, and then you would discover that he had already known about this and had discussed it, and often in an original or creative manner. One of those subjects was racist alienation, which was done without conceptualization, but which Du Bois wrote on extensively and brilliantly.

Charles Cooley was a contemporary of Du Bois at the time he wrote *The Souls of Black Folk* and when he was developing his scientific sociology. Cooley, an economist and early social psychologist, developed a conception of the "looking glass self," which has become a staple of social psychological theory. In Cooley this concept refers to the way an individual interacts with others in a society, and how, from this interaction, he/she assimilates and internalizes culture and develops an identity and sense of self. Du Bois was saying something similar, when he remarked in his turn-of-the-century book on "always looking at one's self through the eyes of others." But Du Bois, who may or may not have been influenced by Cooley, was saying something more complex and more profound than Cooley. Cooley was talking about the interaction of people in some kind of normal fashion. But Du Bois's discussion of Black people interacting with others was about Black people interacting with people who had contempt and pity for them who did not want them to develop a healthy identity, a healthy sense of self: "a world which yields him no self-consciousness." Cultural anthropologist Ruth Benedict once wrote, "we are handicapped in dealing with human society so long as we identify our social normalities with the inevitable necessities of existence."[4] What Du Bois understood about Blacks in 1903, and even years before, was that the "social normalities" that Blacks had to face and interact with every day were, in fact, "social abnormalities" (something he wrote about extensively without this kind of conceptualization). As a consequence of their own racism, which affected their mind, character, and morality, Du Bois believed that Whites, as racists, had a strong streak of pathology and abnormality in them that they sought to invest (through projection, as present-day psychologists would say) in Black people. They also sought to invest the abnormalities of their racist images of Black people in Black people, so that Blacks would accept these defilements as their own and as their sense of self. Having to deal with this kind of psychological assault daily, and over centuries, Black people had to have "dogged strength," especially to avoid fully succumbing to this assault and believing the vile things that white people said about them.

As Du Bois saw it, the racism of white people made them an alienated people. They were first of all alienated from themselves. Their racist fantasies about themselves, their white supremacist fantasies, took them outside and away from their own humanity. Believing that they were gods or godlike, Whites as racists engaged in cruelty and committed abuse against Black people that further augmented their alienation. Being racists and engaging in racist practices also alienated white people from America and what it stood for. As Du Bois saw it, America was bigger than white people, as it was bigger than any people or individuals who lived in the country. America was sui generis, what people imbibed when they lived in America. Du Bois had a strong affinity for American ideals and the America of those ideals, which was reflected in his comment of 1903 that "he would not Africanize America, for America has too much to teach the world and Africa."

White people had done a great deal—initially—had done the most to establish the ideals of America and what it meant. Du Bois, too, would have said, as he did so many times, in so many ways, that America meant or stood for human dignity, individual rights, equal rights, individual and equal opportunities, and justice, all of which constituted the ideal and practice of freedom. This conception of freedom was universal, applicable to all Americans. Having established

America's universal freedom, Whites certainly knew of it. But they could not effectively live up to it or effectively pursue it because of their racism, their slave laws and slavery, their racist laws and racist segregation, and their racist abuses of power. These were all things they threw at Black people to keep them fastened down at the bottom of American society, so that Whites, as James Baldwin once said, would know where the bottom was, the structural bottom and the social bottom, and which direction was the path of aspiration and social progress, or progress toward freedom. But Du Bois saw another significant form of White alienation from America. Whites took American ideals, the ideals of freedom, and used them to oppress Black people, to enslave and exploit them, to segregate and exploit them, and to deny them dignity, individual rights, equal rights, individual and equal opportunities, and justice, and, generally, freedom in America. Whites claimed they had an individual right—an equal right—to own Black people as slaves. They had the individual and equal right to deny Black people rights, equality, or opportunities. All of this promoted injustice against Black people. Whites, as racists, bent, twisted, and perverted American ideals, American universal freedom, and America in relation to Blacks. This perversion induced and encouraged their psychological and social assault against Black people. It also induced and encouraged their psychological and social assault against America and what it stood for. As racists, white people acted in an *anti-American* or *un-American* way toward Blacks and America.

As racists, Whites did not want America, or Americans, or American society, or American culture, or American civilization. Motivated by their racism, what Du Bois would have called white supremacy, or race prejudice, or color caste, but which I would call white supremacy/ebonicism, and which interpenetrated their abstract and practical American thinking, Whites wanted, in a compulsive manner, *White racist America*, *White racist Americans*, *White racist culture*, *White racist society*, and *White racist civilization*. Perverse political and social thinking was a significant part of White alienation in America.

White people, as Du Bois saw it, and as I have been discussing it in these pages, were also alienated from Black people. This was predicated on their being alienated from the humanity of Black people. Their racist beliefs converted Black people, in their minds, into nonhumans, subhumans, animals, or creatures. These were all fabrications of their mind, showing the irrationality, abnormality, and immorality of their thinking, the irrationality, abnormality, and immorality of relating to people this way in order to make themselves feel good, to feel like somebody, or to feel worthy. The deprivation and misery of Black people equaled the elevation and happiness of white people. It was a warped and dehumanized way of thinking. And white supremacy/ebonicism made most white people think this way.

As I said, as Du Bois knew and also said in many ways, Black people interacted with the pathological and abnormal side of white people throughout their history in America. Only infrequently did they get a chance to interact with and deal with the rationality or intelligence of white people or the humaneness or morality of white people. This made life for Black people extremely difficult and intimidating and dangerous. White people, thinking of themselves as gods or godlike, and also guiltless, innocent, and nonresponsible in their racist, fanciful, delusory, and alienated thinking and also thinking of themselves as being just and fair because they were white, would not be capable of understanding Black reactions to them: their suspicion of them, their hostility toward them, their skepticism about them, their disdain for White explanations, their desire to avoid Whites or to have as little to do with them as possible. Whites would be affronted by these Black responses and might respond violently to them; in any case Whites would think pejoratively of Blacks' responses as the kind of reactions expected of lowly nonhumans or subhumans or would, without conscience, use them as justifications to exclude and segregate Blacks.

An insight that Du Bois had, and which again took him beyond Cooley's thinking, was that Black people not only had to interact with the alienation, pathology, and immorality of Whites, but the alienation, pathology, and immorality of American culture, institutions, and society, with which Whites invested them and American civilization, with which they also interacted. With their dominant position in American society and with racist motivation and racist power, Whites mobilized the entirety of America against Blacks, in the form of White racist America, to make the latter play a role in helping to shape the mind, personality, and behavioral responses of Blacks. And this was not just in their childhood and youth, but throughout their entire life. Cooley's "looking glass self" referred to childhood and youth interaction, and only with a limited number of others, primary group people (another of Cooley's conceptualizations), and not with an entire society or entire civilization and not for life. Having to deal with an alienated society and civilization, which were mobilized against them to assault their psychology and being, daily and over their entire lives, literally required Blacks to develop a doggedness of strength and spirit.

It was also required to enable Blacks to deal with their own alienation. Whites, with their ebonicistic, racist beliefs and social practices denigrated black and blackness, racial characteristics, and also Black and Blackness, ethnic traits, or Black culture and social life, making it difficult much of the time for Blacks to identify positively and totally with blackness or Blackness. There were times when Blacks wished they could escape their skin color and other racial characteristics. And there were aspects of their culture or social life that were undeveloped or unsophisticated, of which they might be ashamed. Educated Blacks might be ashamed of the way that other Blacks spoke English, still showing the effects of slavery, the lack of education, and the continuing Black dialect speech pattern. Blacks who were very light in color would exhibit strong alienation from blackness and Blackness, and some, light enough to pass for white, would act on their alienation in an extreme manner and pass for and live among Whites, even marrying and raising families among them. This life meant also having the worry of being recognized or found out or of their children being born with a darker complexion.

Some Black middle-class people (and historically, it has usually been individuals from this class) have exhibited alienation from blackness and Blackness in a peculiar manner. They have called themselves African, or some derivation, such as Africo-American, or Afro-American or, as a number of Black middle-class people do today, African American. The ancestors of the Black slaves in America did not call themselves Africans. That was the name of the continent, but the name had been provided by people outside it.[5] The ancient Romans and the Europeans who came after them called it Africa, and then the rest of the world did. The black people on the continent did not know that name and therefore did not use it as a name to identify themselves and, indeed, had no name for the land mass they lived on and therefore no continental identity. What they had were national names, or tribal or ethnic names, clan names, or family names. These were the kinds of names that the ancestors of Black people had when they were brought to British colonies as slaves from the large continent. This was when some of these people heard the words *Africa* and *African* for the first time, but they did not hear them often, because their captors and enslavers and the white people they would live among called them by other names as well, which they heard more often, such as *Guineas, negro, slave,* and later, mainly in American history, *colored* and *nigger.* *African* was a name seldom used by Whites, because they did not want Black slaves or other Blacks in America having an identity beyond color and race or the slave identity. And the mass of Blacks, Black slaves, seldom if ever heard the word *African.* But it would not have meant anything to them anyway, because it was never a name they had for themselves. The names they had were lost in the slave trade and slavery, and they were therefore open to other names. And Whites gave them many names, which grew out of their racist assumption that they could treat Black people any way they wished, which entitled them to call them anything they wished, which also included for Black men, and often, the term *boy.* Black slaves countered that last name with the word and name of "*man.*" British men had expressions like "good Scot, man" or "Great Scot, man" and used the word *man* frequently in speech. Black male slaves imbibed the word *man* and used it in speech among themselves, and even more so when they were no longer slaves in America. To this day, Black men and Black women use expressions such as "hey, man," "what's up, man?," "dig, man," "what's happenin', man?," or "what's shakin', man?"

Living in the northern part of the United States between the later eighteenth and early nineteenth centuries, it would have been possible occasionally to hear the word *African*; some white person might have used it, or some Black person might have. But the word *African* struck a fear in some northern Blacks because they thought that Whites would interpret their use of the word and name *African* to indicate that they did not belong in America and did not want to stay here. Those individual Blacks who wanted to return to what the world knew as the African continent, would call themselves African, hoping that some white people would help them return to the continent or, at least, to get out of America. And the idea of emigration was born in Black history.

The word *African* also found its way in the name of some of the churches or other Black organizations in the latter eighteenth and early nineteenth centuries. But the people of these institutions or organizations, as their correspondence, or publications indicated, did not call themselves Africans. That was seldom done. They usually called themselves Negroes or Colored, while keeping the name African in institutions and organizations. But the name *African* was taken out of most Black institutions and organizations years before the mid-nineteenth-century war,[6] because of the presence and activities of the American Colonization Society, established in 1817 by prominent southern and northern Whites to try to induce nonslave Blacks, mainly northern nonslave Blacks, to leave the country and ultimately to go to Liberia, a country the Society had established in 1822, with white sponsors picking up the tab. Thousands of Blacks left the United States over the years, but most of them were former slaves whom their masters set free on the condition that they go to Liberia.

The American Colonization Society failed to get most northern nonslaves Blacks to bite on their financed deportation plan. Instead, they attacked it, from the pulpit, from other institutions, and also in their new periodicals. They attacked it, or rejected the American Colonization Society in a more subtle way, by removing the name *African* from most of their institutions and organizations. The name *African* struck a fear again. The same fear that had visited before: the fear that Whites might interpret the Black use of the name *African* as an indication that they did not want to stay in America and wanted to get out. Northern Blacks in the early nineteenth century made it clear that they and other Blacks, including the Black slaves when they were released from that institution, would stay in America.

So why did northern Blacks make use of the African identity? Because they were alienated from blackness and Blackness, more the former than the latter, and in a couple of ways. They were alienated from the White understanding and projection of blackness, which was denigrated all the way, putting black people or Black people in a nonhuman or subhuman category. This was healthy alienation by Black middle-class people and other Blacks in America, and it has been a healthy alienation throughout their history in America. There was also alienation from a color or racial identity, on an exclusive basis. This was healthy alienation, too. But it led to some northern Blacks reaching for some kind of historical or cultural identity like white people's in America. They took the name and identity of African. It was an act of defiance, showing anger and belligerence. It was an attempt to attain a positive identity in a country that under White racist control would not give them or other Blacks one. But the fact that the northern Blacks who used the African identity used it primarily in their institutions and organizations and not for themselves indicated that the name and identity of African was something that they were not that comfortable with, that they deep down did not really believe was their identity. There was a deep recognition that a lot had been lost over the centuries: connections, cultures, and affinities to the homeland of their ancestors, which they could not really claim comfortably, realistically, for themselves. Even if they came to accept, as some others in America did, and as the world did, that the large island continent south of Europe was Africa and that the black people who lived there were Africans, the very best they could do, given the history of their ancestors, the horrendous physical, cultural, and social destruction that occurred among them by a centuries-long slave trade, and the continued destruction of the same under centuries of chattel slavery, would be to claim that they were of African descent, descendants of people that they and others in America and the world regarded as Africans.

Since the nineteenth century, most Black middle-class people and other Blacks in America have called themselves—and this was true up to the 1960s and 1970s—Negroes or Colored people, Negro Americans or Colored Americans, and, sometimes, publicly, black Americans or Black Americans. The words *Negro* and *Colored* meant black and Black in America, to white people and Black people, but Whites, over the history of Blacks in America, showed hostility to Blacks who publicly projected or lauded their blackness or Blackness. This was done in the 1920s but then faded away again. It was done again in the 1960s and 1970s and thereafter, when Blacks from all Black social classes proclaimed that they were black in color and race and also proclaimed that they were Black culturally and socially, without understanding that the latter conception of Black or Blackness were references to ethnicity, not race or color. Black people had always thought of themselves as being black in America. Their eyes told them that they were generally of dark hue or had other similar racial features. They had no problem with their black/dark color. They had a problem with the way white people interpreted and projected black and blackness. The black race in America, descendants from slaves brought to America, evolved into an ethnic group, without a consciousness or understanding among themselves that this was happening, because *ethnic* and *ethnicity* were not words that were available to them to clarify that and would have been attacked by Whites if they had used them, because Whites did not want them to have an identity based on history or culture. But black people continued to evolve into Black people and continued to build and evolve their Black cultural and social life. Finally, in the 1960s and 1970s, they started calling themselves Blacks, and their culture and social life Black, but without fully understanding what they were doing, because they did not have the concepts of *ethnic* and *ethnicity* to help them fully understand that they were an ethnic group in America, like the other ethnic groups that existed in the country.

For some Black middle-class people, even this new lauding of blackness and Blackness, with the latter implying ethnicity, which some of them well understood, was not good enough. In the 1980s and continuing in the 1990s, they have been trying to convince Black people that they are Africans, which they usually phrase African-American, the full hyphenated name, as if they were afraid just to say Africans, as other groups would say just Jews, Germans, Italian, Polish, or Irish, with *American* being assumed. This shows that these Black middle-class people, like Black middle-class people before them, do not really regard themselves as Africans, especially when it is considered that they just as often call themselves black and Black. In the late eighteenth and early nineteenth centuries, Blacks put *African* in names of institutions and organizations, but usually called themselves Negroes or Colored people. The same pattern of behavior, slightly modified, exists today, and for the same basic reason: the acute alienation from any color or racial identity or any identity that seems to suggest or imply that kind of identity, even a positive black identity or a positive Black ethnic identity.

It would be some individuals among the Black middle class today that I have been talking about, who would drop the name of Du Bois, who would quote and praise him and praise *The Souls of Black Folk* and call it a classic. But Du Bois would be critical of these people calling themselves Africans or African Americans. He could accept African descent, Black people of African descent. But in *The Souls of Black Folk* he said to Black people, knowing that some Black people at the time were using the names Afro-American, Afri-American, and Aframerican, that they should not seek to "Africanize America"; this was also a way of saying that Blacks should not think of or call themselves Africans. He made it clear what he thought the historical, logical, and proper names of Black people were, given their history and life in America. He said they were Negroes and Americans, or Negro Americans. He wanted these two identities to be positive ones for Blacks and give them a truer self-consciousness, a truer self, "to merge this double self into a better and truer self." He said in his writing that he wanted Blacks to be able to call themselves Negroes and American or Negro American "without having the doors of Opportunity closed roughly in [their] face."

The identity *Negro American* translates *Black American*. And most Black people today consider themselves, as Du Bois had said they should, as Black people and Black Americans. Some polls have recently been taken asking Black people whether they thought they were Africans or Black people. Always the majority had replied that they were Black. An ABC News–*Washington Post* poll of 1989 learned that 66 percent of Blacks polled said they preferred to be called Black while 22 percent of Blacks polled rejected that identity.[7] The 1990 poll of the Joint Center for Political and Economic Studies had the following results: "Specifically, 72 percent of young Blacks (18–29 years old) preferred Black instead of African-American, as did 81 percent of Blacks ages 30–40 and 83 percent of Blacks 50 and older. Additionally, the vast majority of Black men and women 72 and 85 percent respectively—preferred to be called Black."[8]

In a poll of 1994, conducted among southern Blacks by the Center for the American South on the campus of North Carolina University at Chapel Hill, the following results were obtained: "Respondents to the poll taken . . . were asked what race they considered themselves to be. Among Black Southerners, 66 percent used the term 'Black' and 29 percent used 'African-American.' "[9]

This latter poll first of all shows that there is not much understanding that Black people, the descendants of what can be called African slaves, are an ethnic group in America. All three polls clearly show that Black people, after centuries of having their color, race, and humanity assaulted, are not alienated in any serious way from their blackness and Blackness; they show strong affinities to both. Total affirmation was not always possible and was even dangerous. But historically, Blacks were always more positive than negative about their blackness and Blackness, as recent evidence confirmed. Historically, and overwhelmingly, Blacks have always been alienated from White racist views of blackness and Blackness, and this has always been healthy alienation.

Blacks have also always been alienated from White racist America. This was the America that excoriated their color and race, that denied their humanity, that ridiculed their culture and social life, and that sought diligently to keep them from having a positive identity of and for themselves. This alienation was healthy and helped to insulate Blacks from the worst psychological and spiritual ravages of racism. This positive alienation also played a role in black slaves developing their own culture and social life in America and their clinging to blackness and Blackness in positive ways, which would one day make a full Black ethnic identity possible. Du Bois had recognized how Black people had been alienated positively from White racist America, enabling them to resist it, even if not totally and at all times. Du Bois wanted them to continue in alienation and resistance. Two statements in his 1903 writing indicated this: "He would not bleach his Negro soul in a flood of white Americanism," and "for he knows that Negro blood has a message for the world." But the most descriptive comments ever made about how Blacks were alienated from and resisted White racist America were made by Frederick Douglass in a Fourth of July speech he made in Rochester, New York, in 1852, primarily before a white audience:

> What, to the American slave, is your 4th of July? I answer; a day that reveals to him, more than all other days in the year, the gross injustice and cruelty to which he is the constant victim. To him, your celebration is a sham; your boasted liberty, an unholy license; your national greatness, swelling vanity, your sounds of rejoicing are empty and heartless; your denunciation of tyrants, brass fronted impudence; your shouts of liberty and equality, hollow mockery; your prayers and hymns, your sermons and thanksgivings, with all your religious parade and solemnity, are, to him, mere bombast, fraud, deception, impiety, and hypocrisy—a thin veil to cover up crimes which would disgrace a nation of savages. There is not a nation on the earth guilty of practices more shocking and bloody than are the people of the United States, at this hour.[10]

Implied throughout his comments was Douglass's strong affinity to America, to American ideals, and what America stood for, which he said Whites had assaulted and committed crimes against, as reflected in the way they had treated Blacks, but also in the way they had assaulted and perverted American culture and social life.

Douglass, like Du Bois later and like most Black people throughout their history in America, was alienated from and rejected White racist

America but had strong affinities to America. Black slaves also had such affinities, as reflected in the way they mixed European-American cultural traits with the cultural and social traits retained from Africa to create the new Black culture in America.

But the real affinity of Black people, as slave or nonslave, was to the America of the future—the real and actual America of ideals. This was the future to which American ideals pointed. Nonslave Blacks in a more conscious way, but also Black slaves too, less consciously and with less understanding of what they were doing, wrapped themselves up in America's ideals. This helped them claim America as their own, as their birthplace with birth rights. This helped them understand the illegitimacy of White racist America and gave them, on a continuous basis, the motivation, the justification, and the inspiration to fight that America and to struggle to bring in the other, ideal America, which most Whites kept blocking from sunlight. American ideals, so full of and rich with humanness, humaneness, dignity, magnanimity, nobility, morality, and spirituality were absorbed by Blacks who wrapped themselves in them, augmenting the humanity, dignity, morality, and spirituality that Whites with racism, racist segregation, and slavery tried to suppress or destroy.

But this they had not been able to do. The proof was in the 1950s and 1960s, when Black people, after suffering at the hands of Whites for centuries, made their largest and most effective struggle for liberation, an action of great distinction in human history. A psychiatrist and a psychologist saw this heroic and miraculous thrust, and the dogged, resilient, and heroic character of Black people that it all required: "The powerful thrust of the black liberation movement dramatically testified to the courage, determination, and resourcefulness of masses of blacks—qualities that could arise only from psychological health, not pathology."[11]

America had a friend in Black people, and Black people had a friend in America, that is, the America of its own ideals and the America that knew who and what it was: freedom. This America helped Blacks to survive, helped them consciously and determinedly to alienate themselves from White racist America, and helped them, along with Black culture and Black social life, to mitigate the damage of the negative alienations, from within and without, and the negative alienated responses to them. The ideal America, the America of the future, nourishing Black humanity, Black dignity, and Black morality and spirituality helped to keep Black people keepin' on with resolve and direction in the country.

4.

The Experiment That Never Was, 1783–1883

An archetypal image of Americans is that they are a pragmatic people who like experimenting. When something doesn't work, an idea, a program, or an institution, Americans, as the leitmotif has it, will create or accept a new idea, a new program, or a new institution and will experiment with it to see if it works. If an experiment succeeds, there will be a new fixture. If there is failure, then another experiment will be conducted. Images of pragmatic thinking and practical experiments are locked in history, culture, and social life, and also in the heads and gut reactions of Americans to continue perpetuating the images and the practical experimental behaviors through history.

The American nation-state, erected initially in 1783, as a confederation, then changed into a federal republic in 1787 and officially established as the new entity in 1788, began as an experiment. White historians and political scientists, especially, but also white politicians and journalists and other Whites, have described this experiment as an experiment in political democracy and democratic government. The fact that the country was racist, segregationist and exclusionary and had slavery, the fact that white women had no political rights and few civil rights, (true also of most Blacks who were not slaves), and the fact that Black slaves had no legal rights of any kind should suggest great caution in talking about an experiment in democracy.

Whites, however, have exhibited very little caution in this matter throughout their history in America. And one would be able to see that racism of several forms, but particularly white supremacy/ebonicism, has played a large role in Whites' abandoning caution and also in their colossal denial of political reality to be able to accept and project, as Frederick Douglass would say, "a fascinating delusion" rather than "a palpable reality."

Another major reason for abandoning caution is the overriding legendary image of Abraham Lincoln. The latter is the most written on and the most beloved historical figure to be found in the pages of history books and among white Americans. He has a powerful cultural image as a democrat. Many historians turn especially to Lincoln's Gettysburg Address to chant their praises of Lincoln as a democrat and to offer "proof," some of Lincoln's own words, that America is a politically democratic society and that it had begun as an experiment in political democracy and democratic government. The choice and validating words that historians like to cull from Lincoln's address and project publicly are the following: "Four score and seven years ago our fathers brought forth on this continent, *a new nation, conceived* in Liberty, *and dedicated* to the proposition that all men are created equal."

These words actually convey an image of America being created as a liberal democratic society, that is, one with individual liberty (liberal political idea) and equality (democratic political idea). But Lincoln, like most Americans of his day, and to this day, Black or White or other Americans, did not distinguish between liberalism and democracy. These words today, as in the past, are used interchangeably, but they have never meant and are not the same.

But one has to wonder what was running through Lincoln's mind when he talked about America being conceived in liberty and equality. What would a Black in the audience have been thinking, what would a Black have said, if asked to comment on the speech? If Frederick Douglass had been there, or Mary Stewart, or Sojourner Truth, or Reverend Daniel Payne, they would have reminded the president that America had slavery when the new nation was formed in 1783 and modified in its new inaugural in 1787. And that the new federal Constitution had sanctioned this slavery, without ever mentioning it. And, of course, had it been mentioned in the document, could it have been said in the Preamble to the Constitution, that the country had been brought into existence "in order to create a more perfect union," and "liberty . . . and justice for our posterity"? At the time of the formulation and ratification of the Constitution, it was believed by Whites that Black people would be slaves in America in perpetuity, or forever. And it was believed by white men that white women would never obtain the franchise or hold public office.

The way the American nation-state came into existence and the way Lincoln and other Whites have described its inauguration differ vastly from each other. One is a fanciful construction devoid of reality, and the other is painful reality, the kind that Whites, when functioning as racists, consciously or unconsciously, deny, and do not wish to deal with. The late Black historian Nathan Huggins even talked about political tyranny being ushered in with the American nation-state, because of the existence of slaveholders and slave laws and the maintenance of Black chattel slavery in the country:

> Though tyranny is a word that few Americans would apply to our nation's history, I merely follow the Founding Fathers' understanding of that word. To them a government that was a tyranny did not rest on the consent of the governed, did not honor a person's natural rights to life, liberty, and property. They drafted "bills of rights" to protect themselves against tyranny. People must be free to speak, gather together, and share their ideas and opinions. They should worship as they please. Their persons and affects should be free from arbitrary search and seizure. Accused of crime, they should get a speedy trial by an impartial jury; and if convicted, they should not be subject to cruel and unusual punishment.
>
> By their own standards, the governments they designed would tyrannize black people, slave and free, as well as whites who would champion their cause. That the Founding Fathers may not have admitted to tyranny matters very little. . . .
>
> To call our society by its proper name requires a radical reversal of perspective.[1]

In the case of many white people today, as opposed to most in the past, it would require overcoming the serious impairments that they have inflicted on themselves by their own racism. Other Whites in America are free of racist afflictions or are less impaired by them. But even these groups of Whites today would have distress contemplating the way Blacks look at White history in America and American history under their domination and direction. They have to know, understand, and accept that Blacks are not going to glorify historical figures or a history that have oppressed them. This would be assuming— exposing racist thoughts—that Black people are nonhumans or subhumans and that they accept their own denigration with glee or don't even know that it has occurred or is currently happening. Whites can indeed expect some very radical perspectives that will give them an itch and a twitch and more. And this will be done even when the nonracist side or activity of white historical figures, historical situations, or events are analyzed and discussed in order to provide a comprehensive view of these matters. Even many of the overall views or interpretations will reflect strong racist analyses and discussions because so much nonracist thinking and social behavior in American history and life is linked directly to racist realities and even helps to promote them, for example, the nonracist and American ideals of liberty and equality helping to promote racism, segregation, and slavery in American history and social life. It is not necessary to *look* for racism among white people or in the historical situations, institutions, or events in which they participate. It is usually noticeably present.

The myths and fantasies that white people feed themselves about American history, the way they have made history in this country and want to feed Blacks, ignores, obscures, or denies the horrid conditions under which Blacks have lived in America and which many, if not most, Blacks still live under in the country. This robs, and it is both a conscious and unconscious intention to rob, Blacks of the legitimacy of their thoughts, perceptions, and attitudes and the motivations that spring them into action to address their deprivations. Glorifying Washington, who owned nearly three hundred slaves, Jefferson, who owned over two hundred and twenty, and Andrew Jackson, who owned over a hundred and thirty, would make of these people, for Blacks, *metaphors of oppression*, to paraphrase James Baldwin. It would imply that slaveholding was neither oppressive nor a crime against Black humanity and that the blighted way that so many Blacks still live in America has nothing to do with white people holding them as slaves for centuries. All of this upholds and propagates, with Blacks doing the upholding and propagating, the image of White guiltlessness, innocence, and nonresponsibility and the image that Whites are just and fair because they're white. The myth of the American Revolution conjures up passionate images of newly emerging Americans rising up against oppression, throwing it off, and attaining freedom. It obscures the fact that the most oppressed people in the British colonies were Black people, slaves whom the colonists and the British were both oppressing and exploiting. It also obscures the fact that the colonized British in North America were generally wealthier than the British in England, considerably from exploiting the African slave trade and African and Black slave labor, which rules out the view of the colonized Britons' economic oppression as their reason for rebelling against and fighting England.

Finally, the myth of the American Revolution obscures the fact that the victorious colonists did not have a genuine universal sense of freedom; various forms of racism and slavery continued on in the new American nation-state, as did the significant oppression of white women. And any notion that the war was fought to preserve democracy or to establish the new societal conditions to promote it hangs on the vine of mythology when only a few white men could vote and other people couldn't. When there were Black slaves standing as property to qualify white men to vote and hold office—and then deny the franchise to Blacks, and determinedly so. The writers of the American Constitution wrote muted monarchism into the document. For example, the president could hold office for life if continuously elected, the president conducted foreign affairs and appointed ambassadors and federal officials and could commute prison sentences or pardon criminals. The framers also wrote aristocracy into the document; for example, the president was elected by an electoral college, senators had longer terms than representatives, state legislatures and not the people elected senators, and Supreme Court justices held office for life.

The muted monarchism and aristocracy in the Constitution and new federal system of government were obscured by references to majority voting and elections and even more by conveying the impression in the Preamble that the new federal system of government was rooted in "the people" and that "the people" controlled the government—those democratic images, purposely projected by the Founding Fathers, who were, to a man, as the record of the Philadelphia Convention showed, against democracy. One third of the Founding Fathers were slaveholders. What kind of democracy could they have been interested in? But something else the founding fathers did not do, and which White, Black, or other Americans have not done, is to distinguish between representative government and democratic government. Promoting the former does not mean that the latter is being promoted. Indeed, something very anti-democratic might be operating. The Soviet Union had representative government, coming into existence initially in 1918 for the newly created Russian Socialist Federal Soviet Republic and then for the newly established Soviet Union in 1924. Throughout its existence the Soviet Union had representative government, but that government was at all times thoroughly undemocratic. The Soviet Union showed very clearly that representative government could be used to promote political dictatorship: indeed, *an elected political dictatorship*!

I have accepted, since the 1960s, when I got immersed in the social sciences, that inadequate conceptualization could lead to inadequate historical or social analyses and inadequate historical and social interpretations or explanations. I have for many years rejected the idea that Russia had a revolution in October or November of 1917 (depending on the Julian or Gregorian calendar). To do so is simply not to understand a societal revolution, what is usually denoted by the term *revolution*. And equally bad, it is poor sociology. Revolutions seek to destroy an existing society and construct a new one. That cannot be done in one day, one month, one year, or several years. It takes a lot of time to destroy a society and a lot of time to build a new one. Nothing could be more obvious. But to most historians of Russia, the obvious is not so.

Many historians, political scientists, and journalists argue that a revolution has occurred when state power has been seized. The seizure of state power is the seizure of state power; it might not be for revolutionary purposes at all. Military coups have occurred and continue to do so, not to promote revolution, but to prevent one from occurring or to prevent reform from occurring. Violence against the state, another common description of revolution, is nothing more than violence against the state, which might have as its object a single or multiple reforms and nothing more. Both of these descriptions and others have stood in the way of accurately interpreting and understanding the Russian Revolution. Another great impediment has been ideology, namely, Marxist ideology. According to the Marxists, there were three revolutions in Russia, *in one year*! There were two in the month of February 1917 (or March, again depending on the calendar), the "bourgeois revolution" and the "workers' revolution." Then there was one in October (or November). And then you hear and read of other revolutions in Russia, "Lenin's Revolution" or "Stalin's Revolution," or the "Second Revolution," which is another way of saying "Stalin's Revolution," with the implication that "Lenin's Revolution" was "the First Revolution," as it has been described. All of these revolutions in Russia reflect the lack of concept integrity and concept anarchy, which are endemic in historical writing, as they are in social science writing. There was a revolution in Russia, and only one: the Russian Revolution—not Lenin's revolution or Stalin's revolution; they were simply primary leaders of that revolution. The question is when did the Russian Revolution begin and end? One political scientist/historian, Robert Tucker, has provided a good, cogent answer that unfortunately has had virtually no impact on historians of Russia or the former Soviet Union. In 1977, Tucker argued that the Russian Revolution took *twenty-two years.* "A sociopolitical revolution may, therefore, be an historically protracted process taking place over years or decades. . . . The Russian case illustrates this point. It extended over slightly more than two decades."[2]

Tucker stated in his article that the Russian Revolution began in February–March 1917 and ended in 1939, when Stalin, then the primary leader, finished it off. I accept the twenty-two-year time span that Tucker posited, but my argument would be that the Revolution began in late July and early August 1917, when the Bolsheviks went after state power with which to prosecute a revolution in the country. Actually, the Bolsheviks did not seize state power in Russia—political, military, police, judicial, and penal power—to carry out a revolution. The autocratic state had collapsed and broken up and could not be seized. The Bolsheviks built a state, the new Soviet state, to carry out this effort.

For many years, I have also rejected the idea that Tsar Alexander II freed the Russian peasants with his emancipation decree of February 1861. This is the overwhelming view of the historiography, but it simply is not correct. The decree actually freed the Russian nobility, who had been owners of most of the peasants of Russia, who were serfs. Serfdom had been officially established in Russia in the seventeenth century by laws embedded in the codified laws of 1649 or the *Ulozhenie.* In February 1861, two hundred and twelve years later, Alexander II ended serfdom. He withdrew the state power from the institution, which ultimately maintained and propagated it. This made all former serfs legally peasants. But the tsar did not free the peasants and had no immediate intention of doing that. He wanted to end a centuries-old institution because it stood in the way of fully modernizing Russian society. The tsar wanted the great mass of Russian people to be under authoritative control, only not by the Russian nobility, as an obligatory responsibility. There had always been other traditional forces that had controlled and disciplined the mass of the Russian people: the commune government of the villages, the Orthodox Church, and the Russian state itself. These traditional elements were called upon to continue playing their traditional control and disciplinary roles. A large role was given to the village commune, the peasant village government, which was headed by those known as elders. The former serfs, the new peasants, could not leave villages without the permission of the commune. Alexander II was very concerned that there not be a large movement of peasants from the rural areas to Russia's cities because there were neither institutions nor economic activities that could absorb a large influx.

The tsar, and the Russian nobility and others—as it was actually the nobility and others who drew up the "emancipation" program that the tsar implemented—contemplated the Russian peasants' being free in the country in fifty years. The tsar accepted the plan that the nobility and others worked out, whereby the new peasants would be able to buy half the land of the nobility, who would keep the other half. The land that the nobility sold the peasants was, of course, the poorest they had, and inflated in prices. The peasants paid one fifth of the purchase price of the land, and the state paid the remaining four fifths by issuing bonds to the nobility. The peasants had forty-nine years to redeem the bonds and acquire title to the land. Actually the land purchased by the state was put into the receivership of the peasant commune governments. Peasants made payments to redeem the bonds and to purchase the land to the commune governments, which in turn passed them on to the state. Some peasants might purchase their land before the forty-nine years were up and would be on their way to freedom earlier. In about fifty years the peasants would have land and would be independent farmers to start their road to freedom. They would need political and civil rights in addition to be really free. The tsar, by decrees, expanded on peasant governments, so that many more could participate in government and gain political experience. He also created some new provincial, district, and county governments, all of which went by the name of *zemstvo*, in which peasants could participate on a limited basis with the nobility and the new middle class that the tsar sought to create by the zemstvos and local taxation, that would create agronomists, teachers, doctors, pharmacists, engineers, social workers, and other professional people who would provide social services to peasants and other people in the provinces, districts, counties, and peasant villages. Over a fifty-year period, peasants would steadily acquire political and civil rights, albeit at the provincial and local level, where they would exercise their acquired freedom.

Alexander II's initial emancipation decree, of February 1861, came two years before Lincoln's official Emancipation Proclamation. Lincoln had knowledge of it. It was issued months before the United States and the Confederation of Southern States, or the Southern Confederacy, went to war. The tsar's degree put pressure on Lincoln and the Congress to end slavery, joining the pressure put on them by other European countries that had ended their slavery in the Western hemisphere. The Tsar, Alexander II, was carrying out some experiments in Russia, and these included political experiments, but not a democratic political experiment. These were also social experiments, involving the Russian nobility and people that they formerly owned, working out a different and better social relationship. There was also the experiment of seeing how a newly created middle class would function in Russia. These social experiments were also pressure put on Lincoln and the Congress and others in America.

America's history, in the early 1860s, was running parallel with Russian history, except for the war in America. But Russia had revolutionary elements appearing among the intelligentsia giving the tsar his share of headaches; they protested against some of the changes he was making in the country and also some of the experiments he was conducting, especially the one of trying to work a middle-class into Russia, and a middle class or bourgeois individual and capitalistic ethic. The Russian intelligentsia were interested in Utopian socialism or communal ownership and distribution of the means of production coming to their country, not capitalism, and wanted to experiment with that socialist reality, which would be a political, economic, and social experiment that they hoped would become the total direction of Russian society. Later some of the Russian intelligentsia would want state socialism implemented in Russia.

The United States had conducted several political experiments,

moving into history as a nation-state. One of these was to see if powerful elements in the North and South, representing different economies, different regions of the country, and significantly different
cultural-social orientations, could function in the same national government and country without tearing both to pieces. Another was to
see if a federal system of government, which adjusted power between
a central government and decentralized governments in favor of the
centralized one, could be extended over a vast territory and still attain
the cooperation, loyalty, and obedience of people far removed from
the seat of national government. A third experiment was to see if a
republic, a country where public officials were elected, could be established over a vast expanse of territory when it was commonly believed that republics were most functional within limited city-states
or very small countries like Holland or Switzerland. Similar kinds of
political experiments were going on in Europe, which also saw some
new countries seeking to emerge, such as Italy and Germany. There
was no experiment in political democracy or democratic government
anywhere in Europe, although there was experimentation with constitutional and elected representative government; European aristo-
crats sought to use these to hold onto their power, privilege, and
public deference, and along with wealthy middle-class elements control the movement of other middle-class and lower-class men into as
well as their participation in constitutional representative government.

There was no experiment in political democracy and democratic
government in America either. A constitutional, nationally elected
representative government was being launched. But clearly, a country
with racism and slavery, which denied human rights to many people
and denied political and civil rights to the majority of its population,
could not possibly be democratic. Some democratic devices were used
in the new national (and state) governments, but not to promote
political democracy or democratic government. In the governments
of the federal system, a democratic vote that is, a majority vote, was
employed, but this was not done to promote democracy in government or in the country. It was a device for elites elected to government by a restricted franchise to resolve issues by nonviolent, as
opposed to violent means. Each state in the new country, no matter
their size, had two senators, which made small states equal to large
states in that sense. But under the Constitution and until an amendment in 1913, the Senate represented the states, not the people.[3]
Political democracy is a theory that the people in a society are equal

and have equal rights, and that the majority elects and controls government and changes its composition or direction. Since the majority could not vote at any time during the first hundred years of America's existence, there seem to be no grounds for debate as to whether political democracy and democratic government were being promoted in the country.

A sleight of hand that is often employed to "prove" that democracy was being promoted in America during the first hundred years of its existence has been to say that the Greeks had slavery and that they promoted democracy. Thus, democracy and slavery were not incompatible. To believe that is to toss out all democratic propositions, for slavery is contrary to all of them. The Greeks did not have democratic government. They had representative government. They did not invent that. It had existed long before in the city-states of ancient Mesopotamia. The Greeks invented the word *demos*, meaning, "the people," applied this word to their city-state representative governments, and called them democratic governments. In all Greek city-states only citizens of the state could vote. Slaves were not citizens and therefore could not vote. But the truth about these city-states is that all citizens could not vote. Women were citizens of these city-states and they could not vote. Only Greek men could, and only if both parents were citizens. The Greeks posited the notion that democracy meant majority rule and majority decision. Those were abstract, universal terms that applied to all Greeks (reasonably excluding children from that application). But Greek men refused to apply these democratic conceptions or principles to Greek women. The reason, sexist racism: Greek women were nonhumans or subhuman; they were Non-Others and not entitled to the acquisition and use of democratic principles, let alone participation in what Greek men called democratic government. Ancient Greek government was representative government. It represented men by restricted and exclusionary franchise, functioning, therefore, in an anti-democratic and dictatorial manner, as Greek women especially could testify.

Historians have talked about Western history and Western civilization inheriting the legacy of Greek democracy. These have invariably been white male historians in Europe and the United States who, like the white males of the past that they usually wrote about, called governments democratic which excluded women and denied them human and political and civil rights. In America, white male historians have called governments democratic that excluded white women,

Black men, for the most part, all Black women, and all Indian men
and women. The excluded elements constituted the majority of the
population in America. This was the majority of the American population during the 1830s and 1840s, during what white male historians have called the Age of Jackson, and the Age of Democracy (still
a term in use), with the argument that this was when political democracy and democratic government were really planted in America.
But it was during this planting that most eligible nonslave Black male
voters were excluded from the franchise, especially by white men who
recently obtained it. Two historians recently wrote:

> The democratic spirit failed to carry over to one significant
> class of the population—free blacks. As late as 1820, they
> were permitted by law to vote equally with whites in north-
> ern New England, New York, Pennsylvania, and even Ten-
> nessee and North Carolina. This right, however, usually
> came from omissions in the law and was denied in practice
> until the law itself was tightened. As a delegate to the Penn-
> sylvania constitutional convention of 1837 said on his way
> to the meeting that would disenfranchise free blacks: "The
> people of this state are for continuing this commonwealth,
> what it always has been, a political community of white
> persons."[4]

The two historians, Winthrop Jordan and Leon Litwack, used the
phrase "democratic spirit." But what makes this spirit democratic if
white men wanted only white men to vote? Democratic political theory at no time says that only white men vote or that only white men
hold public office. Nor does it prescribe a majority of white men
voting or a majority of white men electing people to government.
This sounds more like a "racist" spirit working, white supremacy/
ebonicism, but also maleism/sexism, and white supremacy/redicism.
And a person with clear eyes can see all these forms of racism in the
quoted comments above. In the 1820s, 1830s, and 1840s lower-class
white men used democratic rhetoric and public action to gain political
power vis-à-vis white men in the middle and upper class to be able
to join these other white men in the white male political domination
of America. This the Frenchman Alexis de Toqueville did not understand, because he called this white male political behavior *democratic*
political behavior in his book *Democracy in America*, recently cele-

brated by white historians and white political scientists in America to commemorate the 150th year of its publication.

The fact that lower-class white men and other white men were not interested in employing elected representative government to promote democratic government and political democracy was demonstrated by their unison in conventions and legislative bodies to disfranchise most eligible nonslave Black male voters. And there was no thought of giving white women, Black women, or Indian men and women the right to vote. This was promoting inequality, not equality, and was the exclusion and not the inclusion of the majority. This was not a democratic, but an anti-democratic spirit at work, spawned by racisms and a racist abuse of political power, and it made America's elected representative governments function in an anti-democratic dictatorial manner.

Sometimes historians can recognize and admit to these political realities of the Age of Jackson, to the undemocratic and dictatorial character of its politics and governments. Harry Watson recently wrote in *Liberty and Power*: "Direct popular democracy, moreover, was never a reality in Jacksonian America. . . . At its worst. . . . 'Jacksonian democracy' was not democratic at all. . . . White men gained rights . . . but men of color lost them . . . as white men used racist assumptions to justify their aspirations and deny those of nonwhite Americans. . . . Jacksonian equality did not apply to women either."[5] But yet, in his book, Watson still made references to white men being democrats and political democracy and democratic government existing during the Age of Jackson. Such an incredible contradiction! But it remained in the book, indicating how strongly the myth of democracy during the Jacksonian Era hangs on with so many white male historians, who can't seem to let it go even when the evidence they gather and the analysis they provide tells them to do so because the claims are bogus.

But it must not be supposed that white women during the Age of Jackson were interested in political democracy or democratic government. White women were overwhelmingly racists and thought of Black people and Indians as being nonhumans, subhumans, or Non-Others. As racists, they did not want Black men to vote and would have frowned on Black women doing so. But political and articulate white women realized, especially those who were launching the feminist movement at this time, that white women would not get the vote unless Black men obtained it. This angered them. They were

white; they were part of the presumed superior people. They gave
birth to the presumed superior people. That should have entitled
them to something. It did, to various privileges, but not many civil
rights, and to no formal political rights and political power.

White men regarded Black men to be nonhumans or subhumans,
but this was not the way they could look at them all the time. White
racists knew that Black people (or any of their other victims) were
people. There would be no way to look at them and not see human
similarities with themselves. But racists think of their victims most
often as being nonhuman or subhuman and treat them that way most
often; it is a deeply ingrained belief, unconscious as well as conscious,
an a priori response that they believe most of the time. The depth of
this psychological or mental response anchors conscious beliefs and
makes it difficult to alter them to another conscious belief or to hold
one for a length of time. White male and female racists could view
Blacks as human beings, as Others, at times. And it was at these times
that white male racists could see that Black men and Black people,
collectively, could cause considerable political and social chaos in the
country; could engage in or signify threats to the country. White men
in the South, in the first half of the nineteenth century, could never
escape the fear of slave insurrections. When slaves escaped from behind the Cotton Curtain—to borrow a phrase from Black historian
Lerone Bennett, Jr.—they caused conflict between northern and
southern Whites and among Whites in the North. There were also
the organized Black political efforts in America in the first half of the
nineteenth century to protest racism, slavery, and the activities of the
American Colonization Society. Black men and Black people could
cause great political trouble. White men did not feel that white
women would, as their mothers, wives, aunts, daughters, or nieces
and having a stake in White domination of America, be troublesome.
So white men had to contemplate real trouble from Black men, and
Blacks generally, if white women got the vote and Black men did not;
that glimpse they had of them being human beings that told them
this. They took the vote away from many Black men, but not without
decades-long protest about the undemocratic character of the behavior that got more organized as time went on. If white men had to
make a choice between giving the vote to Black men or white women,
they would easily have given it to Black men. Politically oriented
white female feminists knew this and knew that Black men would
have to get the vote before they could obtain it, meaning that Black

men who were slaves would have to get the vote, as ex-slaves. This meant slavery had to be ended, and politically oriented white female feminists realized they had to campaign for the end of slavery. Their right to vote depended on it. Such women were not driven by humane impulses to end slavery or the "democratic spirit" to help Black men get their right to vote restored or to help eligible Black men acquire the vote. Their interest to get the vote for themselves was not motivated by a "democratic spirit." If they had attained the right to vote in the 1830s and 1840s, they would have joined white men in the state legislatures to disfranchise Black voters and perhaps to take the vote from all eligible Black male voters, with no thought whatsoever of extending the franchise to Black women, or to Indian men and women.

So if political democracy and democratic government did not exist prior to the mid-nineteenth century great war, surely they did in the 1860s and 1870s, when slavery was ended and amendments and laws were passed to promote the freedom of Black people in the country. My answer to this is that it is fantasy and delusional thinking. Racism, namely, white supremacy/ebonicism, plays a large part in this fanciful and delusional thinking. But so do the overriding images of Abraham Lincoln as the Great Democrat, the Great Emancipator, and the Great Humanitarian.

Lincoln, as a white supremacist/ebonicist (even if he were not this as much as other Whites in his day) was not, as he could not be, a democrat. But he was not a democrat, not only because of his racism, but because he did not like democratic government (constitutional and elected representation government, yes, but not democratic government). He covered up the rejection by his skillful employment of democratic rhetoric and images, which was the deceptive and manipulative behavior of presidents of the era. Historian Robert Johannsen, despite Lincoln's own rhetoric and what historians have had to say about him, recently wrote that he was not a democrat. In *Lincoln, the South, and Slavery*, he said, for Lincoln, "property" and "intelligence" lay at the basis of government and participating in government. "He argued . . . for government by the country's 'best citizens,' men of property and education who had a reverence for (and a stake in) law and order. Lincoln was a republican, but not a democrat (the lower case letters are important)."[6] Lincoln looked upon democracy as "mobocracy" and a threat to liberty.

Lincoln was also not the Great Emancipator. The Emancipation

Proclamation of January 1, 1863, did not free any slaves. Historians always knew that, but for many, many years would seldom say so and if they did, would not say it clearly. They reflected a racist paralysis of language and description and an obedience to the Lincoln legend that interacted with each other. In 1948, historian Richard Hofstadter admitted that the Emancipation Proclamation had not ended slavery in a book that won him a Pulitzer prize in history.[7] This seemed to open up other historians to say the same.

The Emancipation Proclamation was a military policy, not a statute, and it would take the latter to end slavery. Lincoln had been following in the footsteps of Alexander II, who had issued an emancipation decree. But the tsar's decree was law and went into effect at once. But it was clear to Lincoln and his advisors that what was needed was more than a law. The latter could be declared unconstitutional. This would not happen to an amendment. And besides, as it was understood by Lincoln and others, an amendment was needed as a constitutional principle as the basis and guide for national and state laws. Lincoln favored the Thirteenth Amendment and helped to get it passed through the Congress. Months after his death (after great difficulty) 27 states ratified the amendment to make it part of the Constitution and brought 230 years of Black chattel slavery to an end.

But the Thirteenth Amendment has another truth about it, which historians know but often fail to tell the American public about. There were two Thirteenth Amendments (as there were two Emancipation Proclamations, a preliminary and an official one). The first Thirteenth Amendment, which was never passed by Congress, was totally different from the second. Lincoln and the Republicans in the Congress favored this amendment. It was proposed to the eleven states that were on their way out of the Union, as a way to keep them in; it guaranteed the institution of slavery where it existed but forbade its expansion beyond where it presently was in the West. This amendment would have kept Black people in slavery and misery indefinitely. Lincoln was the only president in the short history and life of the republic to propose an amendment to the Constitution officially and explicitly to sanction and protect slavery. He and others comforted themselves by saying that slavery, contained and prevented from expanding further westward, would die a natural death; there would be time during this period when masters and slaves would begin to work themselves out of their historical relationship into a new one. There is an echoing of Tsar Alexander II's program in Russia in this view.

Another truth about the Thirteenth Amendment yet to be discovered by American historians, political scientists, political philosophers, and politicians is that the amendment was primarily passed for white men and White racist America, rather than for Black people and America. White supremacy/ebonicism was strongly involved. The amendment freed white men from having to compete against Black slave labor and freed White racist America from what many Whites thought was a great burden to it and their own opportunities in the country. Just as Alexander II's decree freed the Russian nobility, Lincoln and the Congress's second Thirteenth Amendment primarily freed white people. The Thirteenth Amendment ended slavery, but it did not free Black people, in the same way that the tsar's decree ended serfdom but did not free the Russian peasants. It simply set them on the road to freedom. Historian Eric Foner recognized that the Thirteenth Amendment ended slavery but did not free Black people: "Unless one means by freedom the simple fact of not being a slave, emancipation thrust blacks into a kind of no-man's land, a partial freedom that made a mockery of the American ideal of equal citizenship."[8]

The abolition of slavery was a necessary step for Blacks to be free in America. This made the Thirteenth Amendment a boost to American history and American ideals. Thus, in this way, was passed for America. But since racism was involved in the amendment's conception, implementation, and passage, it neither freed Black people nor qualified Lincoln as the Great Emancipator or Great Humanitarian. Since he did not endeavor to extend political and civil rights to former slaves or give them land to become independent farmers, he could not be considered a democrat who endeavored to promote democracy. Because he took no interest in extending the vote to women, he cannot be considered a democrat. And Lincoln's image as a humanitarian, emancipator, and democrat are contradicted and rejected by his Louisiana plan, which called for former slaves to be put back on plantations and under the control of the white men who had formerly owned them as cheap contract labor (contracts which most slaves would not be able to read). He hoped to use this as a model for restoring the southern states to the Union.

The Fourteenth Amendment was passed in 1868 guaranteeing the civil rights of former slaves as well as all Blacks in the United States, by forbidding state governments to deny or abridge those rights. In 1870 the Fifteenth Amendment guaranteed former slaves and all

Blacks the right to vote by forbidding the United States Government and state governments to deny or abridge this right. In 1870 legislation was passed by the United States Government enabling the enforcement of the Fifteenth Amendment. Five years later that government passed the Civil Rights Act, enabling enforcement of the Fourteenth Amendment. The Thirteenth, Fourteenth, and Fifteenth amendments established Blacks as citizens of the United States entitled to national citizenship rights and immunities that the national and state governments could not deny or abridge. Legislation was passed to enforce this citizenship and its rights and immunities. These were all contributions to America, its ideals, and what it stood for: freedom. These were contributions that white people made, although Blacks, by helping the United States to win the war and by putting pressure on the United States Government and white people to end slavery and to pass the postwar amendments and laws, had played a large role in helping to move America toward its ideals and itself.

But none of these advances promoted political democracy in America. Only Black men actually got the right to vote. The Fifteenth Amendment was not just for Black men or Black people. As a universal constitutional provision, it applied to all American citizens. Black women and white women were American citizens, but they were not allowed to vote—not by new Black male voters, but mainly by white men who did not want white or Black women voting in the country. American women got the right to vote by the Nineteenth Amendment to the Constitution in 1920—fifty years after the mass of Black men had gained the franchise. Extending the franchise massively to Black men extended representative government and its functioning and reach but did not promote political democracy or democratic government because the representative governments denied equality, equal opportunity, and majority rule. Thus, racism of all the major forms—white supremacy, ebonicism, maleism, sexism, and redicism—was involved in the formulation and implementation of the political and civil rights amendments and their enabling legislation.

There was another way in which racism played a role in preventing vital amendments and legislation from promoting political democracy and democratic government. The restored South, the area where the ex-slaves were, was their immediate target. The white men who exhibited the strongest interest in passing the amendments and legislation were northerners. Some of these men, rich and powerful white men, usually associated with the Republican party and working through it in the White House and the Congress, wanted to plunder the restored South after the war. It was prostrate, exhausted, and defenseless against an exploitative incursion. The northern Whites needed help to fleece the South of its finances, its economic infrastructures, its land, and its natural wealth. They saw that help coming from former slaves. In typical, traditional racist fashion, rich and powerful northern white men congealed around the idea of exploiting Black people for their own gain. What they wanted in the South could not be done without southern Black men having the vote and the right to participate in government. Black men got these rights in return for helping northern white men plunder the South. The former slaves were not always aware of what was happening and how they were being duped and used, though there were those who did, and they took advantage of it for their own personal gain. But political democracy and democratic government were not what rich and powerful white men in the North wanted in the restored South. They wanted governments that could be dominated and exploited. They got what they wanted. And after they got it, they withdrew their support from the Black people they had used. White supremacy/ebonicism returned to full force in the South, and Blacks were overwhelmingly kicked out of the restored southern governments. The kicking-out process was completed by 1877. In 1883, six years later, the United States Supreme Court, in a series of rulings, allowed individuals in states to deny and abridge the rights of Black people, declared the Civil Rights Act of 1875 unconstitutional, took the teeth from the enabling act of 1870, and also declared the United States Government law banning the Ku Klux Klan and its terroristic activities unconstitutional. The full return of national, miasmic White racism, white supremacy/ebonicism swooped down on the Supreme Court and a compliant Congress and White House, and Black people lost their national citizenship and their national citizenship rights and immunities. Whites were back to their full, abnormal and immoral way of relating to Black people. Racism is anti-human being and anti-humanity. It has no interest in democracy and cannot promote it. It can promote constitutional government and elected representative government, but that government, inundated by racism and perversion, will necessarily function in an arbitrary and dictatorial manner toward the people it has excluded and which it will feel compelled to repress and oppress.

5.

The Origins and Legitimacy of Black Power

In 1965, former Congressman Adam Clayton Powell, Jr., used the phrase *Black Power* in some of his speeches. This went essentially unnoticed by Blacks and the media. In the summer of 1966, the phrase *Black Power* was projected by a youthful leader of the Black Liberation Movement, Stokeley Carmichael. This time the phrase hit Blacks, the media, and Whites all at once and with a very large impact. Carmichael kept his phrase before the American public first by speeches and then by a book he published jointly with Columbia University professor Charles Hamilton, which they entitled *Black Power*.[1] For many Black leaders and for masses of Blacks, Black Power became a strident rallying cry. Top Black leaders of the Liberation movement, in virtual unison, flailed against it. White politicians, print and electronic journalists, and many white scholars castigated it; and there was a movement by repressive institutions in America, commanded by white men, to discredit and silence some voices.

I remember seeing Stokeley Carmichael chanting his Black Power phrase, and it might have been the first time that he had publicly uttered it—at least to the American people at large. The evening news made this possible, showing Carmichael at nighttime (the previous night) standing on some kind of platform, with a bonfire behind him with crackling flames and dancing shadows, and with a Black audience about him, chanting Black Power, the audience echoing the chant and cheering him on. The scene was dramatic and emotional, doubt- lessly scary to white people. But it was also scary to some Black people. It was scary to the top Black leadership of the Liberation movement: to Martin Luther King, Jr., the general leader of the Movement and head of the Southern Christian Leadership Confer- ence; to Roy Wilkins, executive director of the National Association for the Advancement of Colored People (NAACP); to Whitney Young, Jr., executive director of the Urban League; and to James Foreman, Chairman of the Congress of Racial Equality. Bayard Rus- tin, protégé of the aging Black leader, A. Philip Randolph, who had been a primary organizer of the March on Washington, D.C., in 1963, strongly opposed Black Power.

Reading about and listening to the opposition of the top Black leadership to Black Power, which the White-owned media widely aired, I was rather puzzled. I was not clear why this leadership reacted with such panic, fear, and hostility and was so willing to join with various Whites to try to discredit the advocates and to silence voices; they seemed to be trying to discredit Black Power and its advocates and to crowd them off the airwaves. By the end of the 1960s, Martin Luther King, Jr., came around to accepting Black Power, not as a political ideal, but as a cultural one. By this time, a number of Black intellectuals had taken up with Black Power and associated it with reclaiming Black history and the Black cultural heritage in America and demanding that knowledge of both be presented to Black people and to Whites and others in America. They also let Black Power in- form and guide their artistic efforts, which spawned the Black Arts Movement among Black intellectuals, including playwrights, fiction writers, poets, artists, and dancers. King found these developments from Black Power useful, invigorating, and redemptive and was sol- idly for them, but for a cultural Black Power, not a political one. What I also noticed was that a number of Black intellectuals had shied away from a politically oriented Black Power as well, in favor of a cultural orientation. That also puzzled me. It was almost as if Black leaders and Black intellectuals were saying that there was something wrong with Black Power as a political reality, something illegitimate about it, and especially the way Stokeley Carmichael and Charles Hamilton conceived it, as general Black community power.

I was no longer teaching at Buffalo State University College, but had entered the Ph.D. program in American history at the State University of New York at Buffalo, formerly the University of Buffalo. I had done a couple years of work there and then had taken a teaching position at a college in Connecticut. It was in Connecticut at my new post that I was doing my serious reflecting on the Black Liberation Movement and Black Power and the reactions to and spin-offs from it. This was all rather natural now, because I was now teaching Black history and American history, no longer Russian and Soviet history (in time, I would resume teaching that). But my knowledge of Russian and Soviet history figured in on my reflections on Black history, and especially on Black Power. I focused on power when I taught those histories, the autocratic power of the Russian tsars and the totalitarian power of the Communist party of the Soviet Union. I also focused on the quest of the Russian intelligentsia for power, with the tsars suppressing their efforts to acquire it but the intelligentsia attaining ultimately enough of it to take over the country. So clearly power was required to get things done; to promote change and development or to prevent or restrict change and development. Russian and Soviet history pointed to a need for power by social groups, something that was necessary to acquire and use. Top Black leaders seemed to be going against what was natural and necessary, and clearly social and of social need.

At Buffalo State I had also dealt with the subject of power in my general social science course. I dealt with some specific forms of power: political, economic, and social power. I also discussed various theories of power with students. One of the theories, Max Weber's theory of power, was widely accepted among political scientists, sociologists, and other social scientists. As highly regarded as this theory was, I felt it was rather inadequate, even offering misleading information about power. It was Weber's theory that power was the means or wherewithal to achieve objectives, even against the will or opposition of others. This theory did not separate power as means from the objectives of power. It did not allow for counterpower that might prevent agents exercising power from achieving their objectives. A flawed implication of Weber's theory was that if objectives were not achieved, then an agent did not have power. This was matched by another flawed implication, that if an individual or group could not stop an agent or agents from achieving their objectives, then that individual or group was *powerless*. How many times could it be read and heard, in the 1960s and even in the 1970s, that Black people were a powerless people in America? And these views were presented with great confidence, as I reflected on the situation, even though Black people had extracted the Civil Rights Act of 1957, the Civil Rights Act of 1964, and the Voter Registration Act of 1965 from the United States government. This meant that Black people had regained their national citizenship, and national citizenship rights and immunities that had been taken from them over eighty years before. How could a powerless people do that? People might not have enough power to achieve objectives or to prevent the achievement of them by others, but that does not mean, as Weber's theory implied, that they were powerless. It just meant that they did not have *enough* power to prevail in a situation. The racist notion of Blacks being a *minority* group in America, so deeply ingrained in the minds of Whites and Blacks in the country, fed the notion of Black powerlessness in America.

When I plunged fully into my study of Black history, American history, and White racism, I also focused on the subject of power, which I knew was involved in all of these areas—had to be. But I didn't know how. In studying these subjects, I learned how power was involved. And the learning experience was eye-opening. Because what was revealed was that white people denied that power played a role in American history or in the relationship between Whites and Blacks, even though white people, in fact, used great power in American history and in their relationship to Black people (as well as toward Indians).

Part of this denial was owing to the exalted ideals of America, which white people publicly lauded loudly and often, convincing themselves that the ideals and realities of America were one and the same or that their espousal of America's ideals was the same as concretely promoting them, which precluded the need of power to achieve the promises and objectives of the ideals. Psychoanalyst Joel Kovel wrote in his book *White Racism: A Psychohistory* that Whites in America "would not have needed such high ideals if part of them had not plunged so low in pursuit of their desires."[2] The constant and strident projection of America's ideals helped to cover up, from Whites, the way they used power in America. Another thing that covered up the existence and use of power, again from the perception and understanding of Whites, was the belief that America's market economy functioned on the basis of rational thinking and rational interests. This, in their minds and feelings, obviated the need of power.

But in the final and most profound analysis, the White denial of power in American history and the White use of power, particularly against Black people, had its origins and continuing life in White racist beliefs, namely, white supremacy/ebonicism. These beliefs said to white people that they were on top in society and Blacks were on the bottom because they were naturally, inherently superior to Black people. It was not a question of power or of a power differential. There was not even any power involved. This, as believed, was just a natural, logical thing. This meant to Whites that they had a natural, logical right to dominate Black people—not with power but with superior innate attributes, which Blacks understood to be superior and to which they, therefore, readily and willingly submitted.

What Whites could not say was that America's ideals or documents such as the Declaration of Independence or the national Constitution with its rights clauses or state constitutions with their rights clauses legitimized their right to be on top of Blacks in American society, to dominate them. These things indicted such behavior and declared it illegal and immoral. It was therefore contrary to what America stood for. So where did Whites get the right to stand above Blacks in society and to dominate them? As said: their racist beliefs, namely, white supremacy/ebonicism, which, in their minds, invested them with a *racist privilege* which, in turn, invested them with *racist rights* against Black people.

What were racist rights? There were a number of them. The first one was the right to deny that Black people were human beings or full human beings. This led to the right to deny that Blacks had a human status or were part of the world's humanity. This then led to the right to deny that Blacks had any human rights. Arguing that Blacks had no humanity or human rights established the right to deny them formal rights, legal, political, and civil rights, because only human beings were entitled to such rights. And this established the right to deny that Blacks had the right to acquire and use power in American society.

Did that mean that the racists had the right to acquire and use power? Did not their superior, innate qualities make that needless? It did. But there were times, it was felt by white racists, when power might have to be used. Blacks, after all, were nonhumans or subhumans; another way of looking at it, they were animals or creatures.

This meant that they could lose control, could get out of hand, and could threaten white people and social order, the stability of the United States. It would require Whites to use power under these perceptions and circumstances. Power was a social necessity at times.

So white people worked it out for themselves in America, worked it out for themselves as racists in the country. As racists, they accorded themselves a racist privilege, which all white people had, regardless of age, class, ethnic group, gender, education, wealth, or region of the country. This privilege gave white people, across these various categories, racist rights. These rights transcended time; they transcended American history. They were rights that were not dependent on American ideals, American documents, or American institutions. They transcended these things and could not be thwarted or suppressed by them. This was the kind of racist thinking that I came to understand from research and study; I saw, looking back on the 1960s, what white people were engaged in when they confronted Blacks in those days, and specifically when they confronted Black Power. Black Power, in their minds, was illegitimate. Their racist symbolism of white being superior, good, and benevolent and black being evil, dangerous, and criminal told them this. To white racists in the 1960s, as was true of white people since the establishment of America, *black* and *power* were a contradiction in terms; they were inescapably a dangerous and evil mix, something that could not be allowed to form in association. It was similar in meaning to white people to the "white" lie and the "black" lie, the good lie and the evil lie.

But of course for Black people to accept the White denial of power in America and their denial of using it or the White argument that Black people were not humans or full humans and were not entitled to acquire and use power would have been moronic, as well as fatal for them in their history and life in the country. These were things that even illiterate and considerably superstitious Black slaves did not believe. Black slaves had known that they were human beings and part of the world's humanity—no matter what white people said to the contrary to deny these realities. A few Blacks, as slaves, succumbed to these deprecating depictions—those who were reduced to Sambos under slavery, and who regarded the deprecations of Blacks to be true. These Blacks were psychologically annihilated by Whites and their racist power and racist psychological assault. But most Black slaves did not succumb to these ravages. They knew they were human beings, just as Whites were, with the same human capacities. Things they did as slaves indicated their human status and humanity clearly to them. They got married (not legally, but after a fashion). Had families. They cultivated and harvested crops. They cleared forests, built towns, mansions, cabins, docks, and roads. They cooked white people food and served them food and did the same for themselves. They raised white people's children and raised their own children. They entertained white people, and they entertained themselves. They built a culture and social life, much of which white people copied, which not only confirmed their humanity but spoke to their originality and creativity.

But Black slaves not only knew that they were human; they also knew they had a right to use power, and precisely because they were human. They used it during the centuries of slavery. They used their physical power as slaves, inherent in their humanity, and which Whites, by using it, affirmed as their human power. Black slaves also used their physical power when they broke farm implements, burned crops, refused to work, ran away, or occasionally killed a master or overseer. But this kind of use of physical power was motivated by something within Black slaves, an inner drive of some kind, independent of white masters and other white people, in no way dependent upon them. And since this was power used directly against white overlords, there had to be a thought and feeling of a right to use such power; a right independent of the overlords. Implied in this right, and in an independent use of power, were an internal and independent sense of dignity and worth and a feeling of the legitimacy of using power.

Black slaves were not powerless under slavery. They could mobilize and use enough power to mitigate the oppressiveness of slavery or extract concessions from it, such as an improvement in diet, some days of rest, or some festive days. But they could never organize enough power, even if they had tried to, to overthrow the institution. Black slaves were the progenitors of Black Power. And they fully understood the sources of the legitimacy of this power. Their own human status and humanity and their own sense of their human rights were primary sources. Their oppressive life was another source. The racist treatment they had to endure, which denied their humanity, was a fourth source, which made them cling to their human status, humanity, and human rights source.

These four sources of legitimacy for Black slave power, for Black Power, as exercised by Black slaves, were the same sources of legitimacy for nonslave Blacks and the Black Power that they devised and used. And they continue on in Black history and American history as authorizations for the organization and use of Black Power.

But there was also a fifth source of this legitimization, which was less known and less used by Black slaves, but which was fully known and utilized by nonslave Blacks and became a source for all Blacks from the 1860s on in the United States. This source was America's lofty ideals of human dignity, individual rights, equal rights, individual and equal opportunities, and justice. This source was initially used by nonslave Blacks and some Black slaves in the later eighteenth century who fought in the War of Independence and made demands upon the new country utilizing the lofty ideals. In the first half of the nineteenth century, the effort was made to plant the American national identity in American history, culture, and social life. This effort ran into grave trouble in the 1830s, when northern Whites and southern Whites began to split away from each other, tearing at the national identity and weakening its hold on the minds of many Americans.

Neither northern Whites nor southern Whites saw the American national identity embracing Blacks, as they also did not see such people as citizens of the country. But northern nonslave Blacks regarded themselves as citizens of the United States and claimed the American identity for themselves and for Black slaves, who they felt would not always be slaves in America and who would one day become citizens of the country and fully recognized as such. This was great optimism and idealism, and it also reflected a great determination. Northern nonslave Blacks, with the motivations and aspirations they had for themselves and for Black slaves, wrapped themselves in the American identity and American ideals. These idealities became sources of motivation and aspiration and were also construed by northern nonslave Blacks as sources of legitimacy for the power—Black Power—that they organized and used in the first half of the nineteenth century. These Blacks also wrapped themselves in the American identity and American ideals for another reason. Both were saturated with humaneness, morality, and spirituality. These idealities nourished and affirmed the human status and humanity of northern nonslave Blacks, which Whites all around them, and daily, were endeavoring to deny and suppress. But American ideals, locked in the minds, personalities, and individual and social behavior of northern nonslave Blacks, prevented a destructive incursion of these annihilating efforts. After the abolition of slavery, the mass of Blacks in America wrapped themselves in the American identity and America's lofty ideals and took the same kind of protection, nourishment, motivations, and aspirations from them. And this included the universal understanding among Blacks, North and South, that the American identity and American ideals fully authorized their acquisition and use of power— Black Power—in America.

And there is something else important to be said about Blacks wrapping themselves up in the American identity and American ideals and what it did for them. It helped, in a very large way, to prevent their significant dehumanization in the United States. White people, acting as racists, have sought over centuries to make Black people accept that they were what white people said they were: nonhumans or subhumans. This has been a continuous assault against the mind, the psychology, the humanity, and the being of Black people. It has been, and plain and simply, White cruelty toward Black people that has lasted for centuries. White philosopher Philip Hallie has understood this:

> Ever since that day in 1619 when a Dutch slave ship brought the first twenty black people to our shores as slaves, America has institutionalized a kind of cruelty so massive, so long in history, so destructive in its effects that anyone who would see institutional cruelty writ large could study that institution with profit. And more importantly the victims of it are still being victimized by it, and are expressing their reactions now in many media and abundantly.[3]

This cruelty, so long and persistent, and often consciously and deliberately inflicted, has done damage to Black people: to their psychology, causing them confusion as to their identity or what is necessary or legitimate behavior in the country; to their morality, even causing confusion about what constituted moral behavior; confusion because when it was performed, it was not acknowledged or respected and was even penalized; and to their spirituality, having an ongoing problem, sometimes mild, sometimes serious, of creating doubts, feelings of insecurity, or fighting back rage about it.

But Blacks, as a people, have not succumbed to the centuries-long cruelty they have had to endure in this country. They have not let white people dehumanize them as a people. Learning how to survive in an oppressive and cruel environment, that is, using their intelligence and creative abilities to deal with this environment, kept dehumanization efforts from having an annihilating impact. Building and living within their own culture and social life has also greatly helped. And the third major practical aid of deterrence or mitigation has been the intense immersing in the American identity and American ideals with their heavy dosages of humaneness, morality, and spirituality.

But white historians and white social scientists, and Black historians and Black social scientists who uncritically ape them, like to talk about the *dehumanization* of Black people; and it is always a kind of confused discussion. The discussion takes place upon the premise of and has as its centerpiece the *victimization* of Black people, which equals dehumanization. But this victimization and dehumanization does not seem to have any cause. It can only be attributed to white people and their racist oppressive behavior against Black people. But white people are rarely mentioned in these kinds of discussions. Racism does not seem to come from them but seems to be located permanently in the atmosphere over America, having no source of origins, not even much reality, as it is not something usually discussed for what it is. For whatever constitutes its destructiveness, from whichever place it comes, it victimizes and dehumanizes Blacks. There are victims, but no victimizers in the usual discussions of Black victimization and dehumanization. This confusion is also caused by the acceptance of the assumption or premise, which the discussion cannot contravene, that white people are a guiltless and innocent people who cannot be held responsible for any deprivations found among Blacks. This kind of hiding away and being silent about white people so that they cannot be exposed or indicted for what they have done and continue to do to Black people is clearly seen in the writing of most white academics writing on Black victimization and dehumanization. The hiding away and being silent about white people also occur in most of the writing on victimization and dehumanization by Black scholars because they usually won't discuss white people to draw them into the discussion as victimizers. Instead, they spend all or most of their time discussing the victimization or dehumanization of Blacks as if it were all occurring in a vacuum; or as if Black people, as innately inferior people, people with low intellectual capabilities, with crippled personalities, and with low morality, have dehumanized and continue to victimize and dehumanize themselves.

Blacks have been victimized in America, but there has been an exaggeration about their dehumanization, by assumption, by intention, by lack of investigation, and by simple copycat scholarship. White psychologists have played a large role in portraying Blacks as dehumanized victims in America (without implicating Whites in any kind of causative role) and in providing terminology for other social scientists and historians to use. A number of Black social scientists and other scholars have accepted this terminology without questioning—the "mark of oppression," or "Black self-hatred," or "Black self-contempt," or "Black pathology." Black psychologist Adelbert Jenkins has chastised white psychologists for their duplicitous role in demeaning the Black psychology, which feeds the arguments used by many about Black victimization and dehumanization:

> The second distortion . . . is the tendency to describe the psychological functioning of the black American in negative terms. This stems in part from the almost complete lack of interest in studying the effective and constructive aspects of the psychological functioning of black Americans. . . . Even where the data suggests strengths and capabilities, these traits are often interpreted as defenses to cover up the deficiencies and insecurities that are "really there underneath."[4]

All the talk about Black victimization and dehumanization covers up *White victimization and White dehumanization* and deflects an investigation of them and a discussion or discussions about them. Still less is there an association of White victimization and dehumanization with a discussion of how these things relate to Blacks. As I have said a few times, white people in America actually believe that they have not been affected, or affected seriously, by the grossly negative behavior in which they have engaged in this country, namely, promoting slavery for centuries, racism and segregation for centuries, and acting in a cruel manner toward Black people for centuries. A self-serving delusion that white people often evidence is that they relate to and treat Black people as they relate to and treat one another (which is often not good). White people, over centuries, functioning as racists, set Black people outside a human status and human morality, so that Whites could relate to Blacks any way they wished, without pangs of conscience and guilt. It is another delusion of white people that they believe they are a people of great conscience, morality, and sensitivity. These are not the attributes they have usually shown Black people in America, and the way they have treated Black people in this country has also shown up in how they have often treated each other. The cruelty that white people have shown Blacks has, throughout American history, also been transferred to Whites. It was a habitual form of behavior that could not always mark its limits, and it drew white people into the abuse. The Irish who came into the United States in the 1840s and 1850s were victims of *racist transference*, not just Catholic baiting. Northern Whites and southern Whites transferred their racist thinking toward Blacks, toward each other, while still executing racist thinking against Blacks, before and during the war between the United States and the Southern Confederacy. Southern Whites lynched other southern Whites annually in the late nineteenth and early twentieth centuries, albeit in much smaller numbers than they lynched Blacks annually.

The white immigrants who came into the United States in the later nineteenth and early twentieth centuries from eastern and southern Europe were called innately inferior people by the native Whites of America and suffered abuse. This threw a lot more confusion into racist thinking. To escape this excoriation and violence, many of the eastern and southern European immigrants were very cruel toward Blacks, to prove that they were just as *white* as other white people in America and entitled to the same White racist privilege and White racist power and rights. The instances of White abuse against other white people represent a different kind of White victimizing and victimization: the victimizing of Whites by Whites, which in itself was a reference to the extensive dehumanization of white people who could victimize white and Black people simultaneously and with similar callousness, hatefulness, and violence and who enthusiastically made institutions function against both groups of people in miasmic ways. But in the end, European immigrants were white, and native white people thought of America as a "white country," which ultimately, after two or three generations, would have to draw the new white people into the fold as equals in racist privilege and racist power and rights in America.

Blacks throughout their history in America have had to observe and relate to White dehumanization. How dehumanized Whites were depended on how racist they were. But racism to any significant degree turned white people against human beings, even against the human status and humanity of people. This is dehumanized thinking. It is also a form of dehumanized thinking always to see a group of people in negative terms; to see nothing but the worst in them all the time, to believe that the worst is embedded in their nature, and to equate their nature with debasement, animalism, or criminality. It is dehumanized thinking, as well as an expression of dehumanized feelings, to believe that a group of human beings do not have sensibilities, such as wishes, hopes, feelings, or aspirations, or that they are incapable of sincerity, sympathy, love, or caring, or that they are insensitive to abuse or pain. It is dehumanized thinking and feeling to believe that physically hurting people, or killing them, is fun or recreation, as southern Whites believed in the later nineteenth and early twentieth centuries, when they beat, lynched, and burned Black people alive. It is dehumanized thinking and feeling to believe that a people love living in a dependent manner, in wretched physical and social conditions and that this is their due. It is dehumanized behavior to act in ways to force them to live in those ways. It is dehumanized thinking and feeling to think that the women of a group are to be assaulted sexually, that they enjoy it and can't wait for it to happen to them. And it is dehumanized behavior to carry out this kind of thinking and belief. It is dehumanized thinking and feeling to believe that one has the right to humiliate and insult other people and to enjoy doing so or thinking there is nothing wrong in doing so or to think that such behavior is necessary or that it is in some way blessed or redemptive.

The descriptions of White racist dehumanized thinking, feeling, and social behavior could be extended further. In Black history, and for Black people, this became another source for the legitimacy of devising and using Black Power. When Whites felt that Blacks were powerless, they would be at their dehumanized worst. They would give vent to all their foul thoughts and passions and oftentimes to atrocious social behavior, as when Whites, throughout much of American history went into Black neighborhoods to carry out waves of violence and destruction, which were usually euphemistically called race riots instead of the murderous and destructive expeditions that they were. Rather, they were like the Jewish pogroms in Europe or the European disciplinary expeditions in their colonial possessions.

But despite the legitimacy of Black Power, which was rooted in

Black humanity, and in reaction to racism, slavery, oppression, and White endeavors at dehumanization—and in the American identity and American ideals—top Black leaders in the 1960s and even afterward were against Black Power. In the case of most of these leaders, as I came to conclude after intense and broad study and looking back on the 1960's and afterward, they were just tied too closely to white people. The White ignorance about the history of Black Power became their ignorance. The Whites' fear of and panic about Black Power became their fear and panic. The fear that White people had that Black people would use their power in retribution became their fear. There was not a shred of historical evidence to prove or even to suggest that Black people sought retribution against Whites. Payback had never been Black behavior in America, that is, behavior as a people; even former Black slaves had not sought revenge. This was clearly an irrational fear and panic on the part of Whites. And top Black leaders, who either knew these historical realities or should have known them, remained silent about them or ignored them and let White irrationalities become their irrationalities. And, of course the threat of losing White financial and public support affected their thinking about Black Power.

But there were other crucial things as well, strictly speaking, having nothing to do with White people. Black Power was a phrase or concept, then a program of action, that came from younger Black leaders. That posed a threat as well as a challenge to top Black leaders, as leaders of Black people. Black Power, with its wide ideological acceptance among Black people, exposed the thin links that the top Black leadership, save for Martin Luther King, Jr., had with the broad Black population and suggested that most of the top Black leaders were leaders or allies of white people, more than leaders or allies of Black people. Black Power came to be accepted, as Stokeley Carmichael and Charles Hamilton had hoped, as Black community power. Top Black leaders simply were not ready to deal with this kind of organized, bulk Black Power. They had fears of not being able to control it and direct it, and these were legitimate fears, because they themselves, with the exception of Martin Luther King, Jr., would not have been able to do either. Black Power broadened the struggle of Black people in America to include political and civil rights but also to include the cultural and social development of Blacks. The development of the Black community and its separate and independent power in America would give Blacks the ability to promote their social and cultural interests in the country on a separate and integrated basis. Most top Black leaders could not get beyond political and civil rights and the social programs that could flow from them and which they conceived as part of civil rights, to ameliorate the condition of Black people and to improve life significantly for some. Black Power pointed Black leaders to the masses of Black people and to their power and development, for which top black leaders, with the exception of Martin Luther King, Jr., who came somewhat around to this position, were not ready.

The confusion and vulnerabilities of top Black leaders in the 1960s and in the 1970s made them susceptible to the White denunciations of Black Power, their direct and indirect declarations that it was illegitimate, and that it was illegitimate for Black people to develop and use group power in America. This was racist cant and racist fear. And this is something that Black people cannot let be their fear anymore; it can no longer be something that restrains or deters them. They need power in America, as any group of people ordinarily need power in any society. As a subordinate group in America, Blacks definitely need group power, effective group power, which can only be if it is organized nationally, regionally, and locally and used in all these ways in a coordinated manner. What Black people need are leaders who understand this, who understand the need for Blacks to develop and use an independent and effective group power, and who understand that it has to be used on a continuous basis, for decades, in a separate and integrated manner, to help Black people develop, prosper, and achieve full freedom in America.

6.

Yet to Learn about Freedom

An image that America has had for a long time, a self-image, and an image that other people in the world have had of it, is that America is "the land of freedom"; that America is a "free society." The implication of all this is that Americans themselves understand freedom and how to make it a social reality for all in the country very well. The reality of the situation is quite the opposite: Americans, generally, have not understood freedom, and they have not made it a reality for all Americans. Former Harvard law professor Derrick Bell recently wrote a book entitled *And We Are Not Saved.*[1] He was talking about Black people not being free in America, not even after the liberation struggle of the 1950s and 1960s and the political and legal follow-up efforts in later decades; these failures were also owing to the White effort to undo changes and progress made. Black law professor Roy Brooks spoke specifically to the White effort to undo or diminish the effectiveness of civil rights laws related to Black opportunities in employment, housing, and education.[2] Among Blacks now the talk is of the subtlety of White racism in America today, that is, white supremacy/ebonicism (but other White racisms as well), not its disapppearance, about the restoration of segregation, and about a serious backslide into a remembered and dangerous past.

But the past is a good place to start to see why a thing is the way it is. A form or forms of behavior come into existence at some point in time, and then, if they continue, they become historical realities that move along a time continuum, into the present, structured in cultural and social garb, and which then move toward and into the future. What came into existence originally in America? The fact that Americans projected a lofty universal ideal of freedom made this the essence of America, what it stood for, and what it was always to stand for, and what Americans should always strive for to make the universal actual in the lives of the American people and in the country. But after establishing the American universal ideal of freedom as the po-litical and social essence of America, White people proceeded to vi-olate and pervert the creation. They established and maintained slavery, inundated the general culture and social institutions with rac-ist beliefs, thinking, power, and cruelty, and promoted racist segre-gation—all of which continuously undermined, assaulted, and violated the ideal and the practice of freedom.

Some historians might wish to take exception to my inclusion of segregation in this trio of contrafreedom elements. C. Vann Wood-ward would be one of them, who popularized the idea among his-torians and other Americans that segregation began in the country in the later ninteenth century, in the South, in his book *The Strange Career of Jim Crow*.[3] Just recently, a former colleague of Woodward's still teaching at Yale University, Peter Gay, reiterated this view:

> Yet, save for some notable exceptions in its small cities, the South had not known racial segregation. Household slaves lived and labored, on a familiar if deferential footing, in the houses of their masters. Some of this intimacy was intimate indeed, an expression in the presence of mulattoes; more visible in the towns than on plantations. In short, for good and practical reasons, segregation was virtually unthinkable. Southern whites and blacks before the Civil War might be described as together but not equal.[4]

These comments reflect a lack of understanding of what segrega-tion was and remains. Segregation is a social practice of domination that involves forced separation or forced confinement: geographically, physically, culturally, and socially. Segregation began in America in the seventeenth century, first in the British colonies and then in

America. British men segregated British women in the home and in other areas of British colonial society. This kind of behavior carried over into American national history. In the seventeenth century, Indians were segregated on reservations. Also in that century, when African slavery was established in the British colonies, particularly in southern colonies, the slaves were forcibly confined to plantations and farms; that is, they were segregated on plantations and farms. This was also true of the Black slaves who decended from them, and who were segregated in these places in the South at the opening of America's national history. This practice continued on in that history with the aid of police forces, called patrollers, to help enforce the segregation.

The segregation was ostensibly racial, obviously racial, but it was racial segregation predicated on and implemented by racist beliefs; thus it was really fundamentally racist segregation, that is, segregation based on the assumption that Black people were not people or full human beings. Similarly the segregation of British and American women was not just gender segregation, for, as it was based on maleist/sexist ideas and maleist/sexist motivation, it was also really fundamentally racist segregation. Racist thinking is by definition power thinking and segregationist thinking, thinking that seeks to dominate, control, confine, and usually exploit people.

Historians have not helped Americans, White, Black, or otherwise, to understand freedom. Most avoid dealing with White racism in American history, particularly how it has affected White people and American cultural and social life and, therefore, the way white people have practiced freedom in America. When historians do deal with racism, it is usually in a brief discussion that is not about Whites, but about Blacks and the way or ways they have been victimized by racism, which is usually discussed in terms of race, not racism. Historians also either avoid or talk sparingly about segregation. The latter is even true when there is a discussion about Jim Crow laws and segregation in the South in the later nineteenth and early twentieth centuries. What discussion occurs is about how segregation affected Blacks. But the discussion rarely turns toward White people, to show how their segregationist thinking and social behavior affected their understanding and implementation of freedom in America. Even discussions of slavery have brought no more enlightenment about how White people believe in and practice freedom in America. Black slavery in the United States is one of the most written-on subjects in

American history today, by White and Black historians. White historians usually write about the institution to minimize its despotism and the despotic behavior of White people. Black historians usually do not like to deal with these matters either, preferring to focus on the culture and social life of the Black slaves, invariably in isolation from the despotic conditions in which this life evolved and which these conditions affected in the forms that it took. Both Black and White historians have thus far avoided, in any significant way, discussing the impact that 230 years of chattel slavery had on White thinking about freedom, their practice of it, and the way they made American institutions practice it. White historians have engaged in mental zigzagging to avoid looking at slavery as I have described, by thinking or writing about it in a way that makes it appear as if it were not an integral part of American history, culture, and social life; as if it were some kind of aberration from the main historical, cultural, and social realities of America. Nathan Huggins felt that White historians generally treated not only slavery, but also racism and racist segregation, as if they were marginal to the life of White people and to American history and society: "Slavery has been seen as a pathological condition, studied as a disorder . . . racism and racial caste . . . have been, in their turn, studied as the 'tangle of pathology' of blacks. . . . Very little thought has been given to the general health of the society that created and sustains them. Society and its historians have treated all these phenomena as aberrations, marginal to the main story."[5]

White historians, by blocking out aspects of American history, so that white people do not have a memory of or knowledge about them or consider them in any significant manner, if at all, help to prevent white people from having to engage in deep introspection about themselves and the history they have made in this country—those aspects of themselves and the history they have made here that are painfully disagreeable to their contemplation. Not having to deal with such matters feeds the racist image and feelings that white people have of themselves, that they are guiltless, innocent, and nonresponsible and that they have produced nothing but benefice for America and all the people in it. Black historians also, invariably and contradictorily, feed these images and these feelings themselves. They rarely write on the history of white people in this country or the history of America. Their writing is overwhelmingly in Black history, invariably in essential isolation from white people and the larger American history. Some talk about Black history as the foundation for a critical evaluation of the history of white people and American history. But this has been and continues mainly to be talk. Thus, Black historians help to marginalize racism, racist segregation, and slavery in American history and life. They do the work of racists and racism without knowing this is what they're doing and without knowing how racists and racism are manipulating them into doing it to keep white people from learning and understanding themselves better and how they have generally understood and promoted freedom in this country.

White historians are fond of using such phrases in their historical writings as "free North" and "slave South" or "half free" and "half slave" in referring to the northern and southern parts of the United States, respectively. All of these phrases were primarily used by northern Whites in the first half of the nineteenth century. Other phrases were used during this earlier time, mainly by northern Blacks and Whites alike, such as "free" Negroes, "free people of color," or "free" blacks (usually spelled in the lower case). Black and White historians have echoed this usage in their writings.

All of this represented uncritical scholarship. Historians have an obligation to be critical in their analysis of historical behavior, to be able to distinguish between fact or fiction, fantasy or reality. They must separate ideals from actual behavior, what is believed or professed from what is done. Take the word *free* as it relates to northern Black people in the first half of the nineteenth century or to "free" Blacks in the South. The last thing these Blacks were was free in the United States. For historians to say that they were, Black or White historians, is to convey the impression that White people understood freedom and promoted it across race and widely in America, that they were living up to the ideals of America and implementing them. The so-called "free" Blacks, North and South, knew better than this. They themselves would have been clearer, as would have their white contemporaries, had they both used the phrases—as mainline usage, and not as infrequent usage, as happened in that day—"nonslave," "nonslaves," "nonslave Negroes," or "nonslave blacks." These phrases would have made it clear to historians that Black people who were not slaves in America did not think of themselves as being free and that they were seeking to be free; this is what their organizational and protest behavior at the time indicated. The different phrases and the political behavior would have made it quite clear to historians investigating these realities of the past that white people were not

promoting freedom on a wide basis in the United States in the first
half of the ninteenth century. This awareness would lead to the logical
critical question, begging for a critical answer: if white people were
claiming that they were promoting freedom in this period, what kind
of freedom was it, since they denied human dignity, individual and
equal rights, individual and equal opportunities, and justice to other
people?

Even so, the clearer phrases, such as "nonslave" or "nonslave
Blacks," were not overly necessary for professional historians to
plunge into critical scholarship and to come up with critical explanations. Their glimpse of Black organizational and protest activities
(to say nothing about the "black laws," i.e., the racist laws), would
have indicated to them that phrases like "free" Negro or "free" Col-
oreds had no validity. This would have led to the first logical step of
explaining why nonslave Blacks used these phrases, and some obvious
answers could have been provided. They wanted northern white people to know that they were not slaves. They wanted them to know
that racist laws passed to deny them dignity, individual and equal
rights, individual and equal opportunities, and justice were illegal and
immoral. They wanted fugitive slave hunters, looking for escaped
slaves in the North or ignoring the freedom papers they had on them
not to mistake them for runaways. They were saying to northern and
southern Whites that America was their home and the home of the
Black slaves, who would not always be slaves in the country. Finally,
they used "free" Negro to hold onto this consciousness, daily under
assault, that produced thoughts of freedom and actions toward
achieving it.

White historians especially have been and continue to be uncritical
with phrases like "free North" and "slave South," "half free" and
"half slave," and the discussions that have flowed from them. The
slave phrases were true and conformed to reality, but the free phrases
did not relate to northern reality in the first half of the ninteenth
century. They actually reflected White self-deceptions and cover-ups
of reality. White historians especially, but Black historians, too, mainly
by neglect in their historical writings, cover up these cover-up realities
of the past for historians and others who now read their writings.
Blind spots in historical analysis are perpetuated by historians who
accept blind spots by uncritical copycatting.

If it were understood that Black people were not free in the northern part of the United States in the first half of the nineteenth cen-

tury, which any historian who looks at the evidence with even one eye would know—then what could the phrases "free North," "free states," or "half free" mean, especially when it is considered that white women at this time had no political rights and only a few civil rights and that Indians in the region had no political and civil rights at all? The only people these phrases could be referring to would be white men. But what kind of freedom did they believe in and practice if they denied freedom to everybody else? It certainly wasn't any freedom consistent with American ideals, which would declare such freedom as being false, as being unfreedom or anti-freedom. White men at the time, as American ideals and their own behavior contradicting and violating these ideals indicated, did not believe in a genuine universal liberty, a genuine universal equality, or a genuine universal freedom. This included Abraham Lincoln, who used the same kind of phrases, such as "free North," "free states," and "half free," and who, like his northern and southern white male contemporaries, believed he had an individual and also an equal right to deny rights and that this was their real notion of universal freedom. This was perverted liberal democratic political thinking, in short, the negation of such thinking.

This of course strikes hard at the colossal mythological images of Lincoln and at the historians who continue to perpetuate them. They really wax angry at remarks that Lincoln was a white supremacist/ebonicist that would not have wrinkled Lincoln, because he himself said he was. He did not say it as often or as loudly as other white men or women said it in his day. But he publicly expressed white supremacist/ebonicistic remarks nonetheless, at times rather strongly. In the 1960s Lincoln's racism was exposed by historians, as America's racism, past and present, was exposed in historical writings. Lerone Bennett, Jr., made the following remarks in 1968:

> Abraham Lincoln . . . was a tragically flawed figure who shared the racial prejudices of most of his white contemporaries. . . . The myth-makers have not only buried the real Lincoln; they have also managed to prove him wrong. He said once that it was not possible to fool all of the people all of the time. But his apothesis clearly proves that it is possible to fool enough of them long enough to make a conservative white supremacist a national symbol of racial tolerance and understanding.[6]

In the 1970s and especially in the 1980s, when the Black Liberation Movement spent its gas after two decades of intensive liberation
activities, White racism returned as a strong force in American society—proving that it had not been killed off. The worst of it had
essentially been destroyed. But the subtle racism that Whites had always practiced in America as well—this form of racist perversion—
now became the main kind. In the 1970s and 1980s and continuing
in the 1990s, this more subtle, perverted racism hid itself in what was
called "conservatism," "conservative" politics, "Middle America," or
the "Heartland." It was nothing that ever fooled Black people. It
only showed them where many, if not most, White people's heads
still were, including many, if not most, white historians. They re-
sumed the tradition of running interference for Lincoln with their
scholarship. They had a serious problem, for Lincoln's racism had
been exposed. Given the interference writing that followed, it was
apparently decided, individually, collectively, or on an unconscious
basis, by simply copying one another, to play down Lincoln's racism
and make it appear as if it were not very significant. Some historians
even took the tactic of saying that Lincoln "outgrew" his racism
before his death.

Let's look at what historians wanted to play down. In one of his
debates with Stephen Douglas in 1858, Lincoln expressed his hostility
to the further expansion of slavery to the West, because he believed,
as he said, that the West belonged to "*free white people*"[7] (italics his).
In those same debates, he also said, referring to the natural endowment or capacity of Blacks in comparison to those of Whites: "In
pointing out that more has been given you, you cannot be justified
in taking away the little which has been given him. . . . If God gave
him but little, that little let him enjoy."[8] In another debate with
Douglas, he made a reference to a speech he had made four years
previously, because he wanted to show Douglas and his white audience that he had held racist sentiments for many years: "But to show
that my sentiments were long entertained and openly expressed; in
which extract I expressly declared that my own feelings would not
admit a social and political equality between the white and black
races."[9] There are the following remarks made by Lincoln in 1858,
and during yet another one of his famous debates with Douglas:

> I will say, then, that I am not, nor ever have been, in favor
> of bringing about, in any way, the social and political equal-

ity of the white and black races—that I am not, nor ever have been, in favor, of making voters or jurors of negroes, nor of qualifying them to hold office, nor to intermarry with white people; and I will say in addition to this, that there is a physical difference between the white and black races which will ever forbid the two races living together on terms of social and political equality.[10]

Lincoln was a racist and did not hide it. But his admitted racism has proven an embarrassment for white historians who want to make him the archfigure of all that America stands for, that is, the archsymbol of freedom in America. As for the historians who said he outgrew his racism, the first Thirteenth Amendment, which would have maintained Blacks in slavery indefinitely, Lincoln's efforts during the first two years of the war to find countries in the Western Hemisphere to take 4,500,000 Black people whom he wished to deport from the country, the Thirteenth Amendment that freed white men and white people and not Blacks, and the fact that Lincoln would not give former slaves land and political and civil rights and wanted to return them to plantations and the control of Whites show that he did not outgrow his racism. Lincoln, like other white men of his day believed in *white male liberty* and *white male equality*, these forms of universality, and not the lofty, genuine universal liberty or equality, no matter how many times or how loudly they said so publicly. This was their understanding of freedom and the way they practiced it. Both of these perverted conceptions of freedom can be defined on the basis of the way white men practiced freedom in America. White male liberty meant *the right of white men not to be dominated, controlled or exploited by other white men, but the right of all white men to dominate, control, and exploit anyone in America who was not a white male, especially Blacks.* White male equality meant *the equal right that all white men had with each other not to be dominated, controlled, or exploited by one another, but the equal right of all white men to dominate, control, and exploit anyone in America who was not a white male, especially Blacks.* This was racist privilege, which white men in America converted into racist rights and racist equality. These were the things that white men understood to be freedom, which was against American ideals and American universality and which they practiced to violate those ideals, proven by the way that they insisted that America's ideals did not apply to Blacks and the way they used great power to deny Blacks rights and equality.

White men also insisted that America's universal ideals did not apply to white women. This presented a problem for white women, of course, but also for white men. There were Black and Indian women in America, and white men wanted to be able to relate to them in any way their racisms propelled them. This presented a threat and a danger to white women to whom white men might transfer this behavior, especially since they related to white women primarily on a maleist/sexist racist basis. White women wanted some rights and guarantees against abuse against them. They did not want to be treated as slave women, "squaws," or "nigger wenches." In the decades before the war between the United States and the Southern Confederacy, northern white women began to organize for their protection and try to obtain formal rights.

The effort to obtain formal rights, civil and political, was a reflection that some white women were no longer content with just the racist privilege, power, and rights that white women could exercise against Blacks or Indians in the country. White men had extended this kind of privilege, power, and rights to white women originally in the seventeenth century, when white men began to abuse Indian, African, then Black women. Under white female fears and pressure, white men, in the seventeenth century and thereafter, projected a public image of white women that placed them on a pedestal: an image that depicted them as beautiful, feminine, gracious, sensitive, loving, desirable, and the like. This contrasted with the public image that white men projected of Black women, whom they considered the direct antithesis of white women: masculine, hard, ugly, unfeminine, undesirable, ungracious, coarse, licentious, and so on, with Indian women being depicted in a similar way. These were racist images being projected: white supremacy projecting the lofty images of white women and ebonicistic/sexist and redicist/sexist racisms projecting the denigrating racist images of Black and Indian women. White men established a racist privilege for white women that invested them with racist power and rights, which could only be exercised against Blacks or Indians, not against white men. But there were white women who wanted rights and equality in interactions with white men and wanted them for all white women in the country. This led to the launching of the feminist movement in the first half of the nineteenth century. But white women, racists like white men, were not interested in genuine universal rights, equality, or freedom. They were interested in a perverted, universal *white female liberty and white female equality.* The first meant *the right of white women not to be dominated, controlled, or exploited by white men, but their right to dominate, control, and exploit all in America who were not white, especially Blacks.* White female equality meant *the equal right that white women had with white men not to be dominated, controlled, or exploited by each other, and the equal right with white men to dominate, control, and exploit anyone in America who was not white, especially Blacks.* This was how white women understood freedom. They understood it in a racist, perverted manner, the right to be excessively privileged and the right to deny rights.

And they knew just like white men the kind of rights they wanted to deny. Fundamentally, they would deny the human rights of Black people and Indians in America; their racist thinking compelled them to want to do this. It meant, then, the right to deny political and civil rights, for nonhumans or subhumans did not qualify for such rights. As I have said, if white women had gained formal political and civil rights in the first half of the nineteenth century, they would have, like white men, invested their racism in the ideals of America and would have used these perverted ideals to deny their application to Blacks. They would have then employed the same perverted ideals to deny concrete dignity, individual and equal rights, individual and equal opportunities, and justice to Black people, would have, in concrete ways, denied freedom to them. They would have done the same to Indians. White women, like white men, learning from them, understood that freedom in America, for white people, meant the right to bend, twist, and pervert American ideals in the interest of white people and against people who were not white. But most white people did not learn about freedom, genuine, universal freedom, and they still have not learned much about it; because most are still practicing White racist privilege and White racist power and rights in the country.

The rule of law, a cherished ideal in America, has not, throughout its implementation in American history, helped many white people understand genuine freedom. The ideal of the rule of law in America was that it was to promote the universal American ideal of freedom. But throughout a long portion of its history, white Americans promoted slave law and the rule of slave law. Throughout virtually their entire history, they have promoted and implemented racist law. These two forms of law made it possible for Whites to engage in legal lawless behavior against Black people (and Indians, and other people of color in the country). The Jim Crow racist laws passed in the American South in the late nineteenth and early twentieth centuries were not dismantled until the 1960s and 1970s, and they are not yet completely dismantled. And where racist laws no longer exist in America, racist thinking and racist practices continue. So when have most white people had a chance to learn about a genuine universal freedom? Most have not had that opportunity. Another way of saying what white people have generally learned in America is that they have generally learned *license*, which is just the opposite of freedom. Frederick Douglass had said that in his famous Fourth of July speech in 1852, "your boasted liberty, an unholy license . . . your denunciation of tyrants, brass fronted impudence; your shouts of liberty and equality, hollow mockery." License means the right to say and do as one pleases, without any thoughts or feelings for others or for the rights of others and without a concern for the consequences of what is said about and done to others. Racism, beliefs and practices, is pure license. White people have practiced this kind of licentious thinking and social behavior against Black people since the two have lived in this country. For centuries Whites, functioning as racists, have thought and acted on the thought that they had the right to abuse people, to humiliate people, to insult people, to deny people, to exclude people, to deprecate the intelligence of people, to assault the self-esteem of people, to profess public hatred of people, and so on! These were not rights conferred upon them by America, but rather by White racist America. The latter even taught them that when they verbally deprecated or excoriated or humiliated or insulted people, they were engaged in freedom of speech, protected by the Constitution, government, statutes, and the courts. What kind of right is it when one has a right to humiliate, to abuse, to insult, to denigrate, to suppress, and exploit? How do such rights contribute to or enhance the public morality? What country sanctions such heinous rights as an ethically and spiritually blighted public morality? America certainly doesn't. The Declaration of Independence doesn't. The Constitution doesn't. But White racist America and a White racist interpretation of the Declaration of Independence and Constitution do, and both with great enthusiasm. White racist America has made white people, functioning as racists, the country's models, in thought and practice, over the entire history of the country of licentious behavior. All this time, they have persistently, irrationally, and immorally charged other people with this kind of behavior, Blacks especially, but also Indians and Hispanic people, in the classic manner of racists projecting onto other people, blaming other people, and then feeling self-righteous, guiltless, innocent, and nonresponsible. But the historical (i.e., past, present, and continuing) White racist licentious behavior, individual, group, institutional, and regional is seriously affecting other people in the country in a different way than in the past. In the past, but also presently, White racist licentious behavior created and perpetuated victims. Now some of the victims are beginning to think and act like their White racist abusers. There are Blacks now, young ones and older ones, who seek to act in a public licentious manner, without regard for anyone. Cornel West has failed to understand this motivation and social behavior. In his book *Race Matters*, read by many white people, he discussed something else that he felt was presently plaguing Black people and getting worse. He called it *nihilism*.

> The proper starting point for the crucial debate about the prospect for black America is an examination of the nihilism that increasingly pervades the black communities. Nihilism is to be understood here not as a philosophic doctrine that there are no rational grounds for legitimate standards or authority; it is far more, the lived experience of coping with a life of horrifying meaninglessness, hopelessness and (most important) lovelessness. The frightening result is a numbing detachment from others and a self-destructive disposition toward the world.[11]

The first thing to be said here and contrary to and in criticism of West's view that the "proper starting point for the crucial debate about the prospect for black America" is that the critical point of departure is not so-called nihilism, but rather white people and their racist history, their racist beliefs, their racist thinking, their racist psychological afflictions, and their use of racist power. In short, the *proper* starting point has to be and can only be with the perpetrators and not the victims. With that said and understood, something can be said about this so-called Black nihilism. Nihilism itself was a form of thought used by the Russian intelligentsia in the 1860s, and it impacted Western European intellectuals. The intelligentsia were beginning to move into their revolutionary posture, and there were those among them who argued that nothing should have legitimacy or authority or be able to invoke loyalty that could not stand the test of reason and science. This was an attack against those things in Russia's autocratic society, which some intelligentsia thought were wholly irrational, such as the Russian state, a very privileged nobility, and the Orthodox Church and religion, which still held power and invoked loyalty in Russian society. Western European observers of this Russian phenomenon misunderstood it and asserted that the Russian intelligentsia did not believe in legitimacy, authority, or even in existing reality. This was the (mis)understanding of nihilism that Western intellectuals turned into a doctrine. West said the Western conception of nihilism was not occurring among Blacks in America. But what he called nihilism among them was not nihilism at all. West did not recognize a disjunctive cynicism that is spreading among a number of Blacks and leading them toward public licentious behavior, within the Black community and without. This, indeed, has something in common with Russian nihilism, which had such cynicism as an integral part of it. But West demonstrated another failure, that of not recognizing how long nihilism had been in existence in Black life, and this was nihilism the way the Russian intelligentsia understood it, but predating them by centuries. This form of Black nihilism went back to the late seventeenth and the first half of the eighteenth centuries, when ebonicistic racism and African and Black chattel slavery were planted in the British colonies. Ebonicistic racism alone, but ebonicistic-inundated chattel slavery, as well, said to African and Black slaves that they were nonhuman and subhuman, which both kinds of slaves rejected, as revealed in their restructuring of Christianity, in their various forms of protest, in their work songs, and in their new religious music—the spirituals. These rejections were also, and clearly, rejections of White racist claims of authority and legitimacy, precisely because they could not be validated by reason, intelligence, or morality. Nonslave Blacks continued their nihilistic rejection of White racist claims, in their various ways, into and throughout the functioning of the new America up to the abolition of chattel slavery. Nonslave Blacks throughout this lengthy period, traversing colonial and nationalistic spans of history, rejected in a nihilistic manner White racist claims of authority and legitimacy. This was done intellectually by oral or written commentary, by various forms of moral and political protests, and also by other practical means, such as building a

Black community or a Black society on the assumption and understanding that Blacks were human beings and that they were intellectually and morally capable of doing so. White racists, as Black slaves
and nonslave Blacks were both to experience, tried to enforce racist
conceptions of authority and legitimacy upon them with power that
was just as devoid of rationality, morality, and spirituality as the racist
conceptions and claims themselves. Blacks were clearly the inventors
of nihilism in America, and their invention and practice of nihilism
occurred long before the Russian intelligentsia devised the thinking,
although the latter were to add the ingredient of science to go along
with reason as joint means to reject the irrational philosophical, social,
or institutional bases or functioning of society. Frederick Douglass's
Fourth of July speech was pure nihilistic rejection of White racism in
America, although, and as was characteristic of Black nihilism at this
time and later, it did not involve cynicism, disjunctive or otherwise.

But there was alienation among Blacks all the years they were nihilistic, and the two were woven together and employed together
both to criticize and reject White racist America, understood to be
the negation of America and rationality and morality. This combination of alienation and nihilism was augmented when social, especially, but also physical science was added to it in the late nineteenth
and early twentieth centuries and thereafter. This integrated and in-
teractive combination of thought and method were part of the Black
Liberation Movement in America in the 1960s and 1970s, strong
movers of it. But in the 1970s and 1980s White racism returned as
a strong force in America, having weathered a strong assault, and it
continues on as an obdurate force in the 1990s. And its continuation
means what racism has always meant to Black people, that most white
people have never understood freedom and do not know how to
practice it. All most really know is license, and that's what they keep
practicing. This has begun to make a lot of Black people cynical about
white people and their capacity to understand and practice freedom.
This cynicism comes through the statement that can be heard among
many Blacks today, intellectuals, activists, and others, that America
will always be a racist society. That means that there are Blacks now,
with the numbers growing, who believe that America's ideals will
never greatly determine white people to behave in a way that America
insists. This is an expression of disjunctive cynicism. But there is nihilism involved here, too, now aimed at American ideals and America
itself. The authors of *Cool Pose*, a study of young Black adults, wrote:

Yet African-American men have defined manhood in terms familiar to white men: breadwinner, provider, procreator, protector. Unlike white men, however, blacks have not had consistent access to the same means to fulfill their dreams of masculinity and success. Many have become frustrated, angry, embittered, alienated, and impatient. Some have learned to mistrust the words and actions of the dominant culture.[12]

This is fertile ground for the development of disjunctive cynicism and nihilism among Blacks, aimed at the ideals of America and at America as well. This represents a new development in Black history—many Blacks turning against American ideals and America. This leads to licentious behavior, inside Black communities and without. And this problem can be laid at the feet of white people in America, who have been great executioners and teachers of licentious behavior, not only on the individual or group level, but also by the way they have made and continue to make societal or local institutions function in a licentious manner, especially against Blacks in this country. Economic institutions, educational institutions, and social service institutions dispensing "welfare" are primary examples of this kind of institutional behavior.

White Americans, as a group of people, have yet to take responsibility for America. Their responsibility, as a group of people, has always been primarily toward White racist America. This kind of history gives America a dangerous future. It is a future that white people can help America avoid, but it's going to require that they learn what freedom really means and what it really means to practice it in the country.

7.

Subtle White Racism

In the late 1960s, the Black Liberation Movement began discernibly to subside. By the early 1970s, it was over. This was discernible, too, and I observed it from my teaching post in Connecticut. And I came up with what I thought were some valid reasons for the demise of what had been a progressive and glorious chapter in American history. The Movement was the greatest internal thrust for freedom that the country had ever seen, and America could recognize and revel in. Most white Americans and White racist America could not celebrate it, though, and could only contemplate with horror, anger, or fear. America could have Black heroes and heroines, but White racist America couldn't.

I implicated the success of the Movement in its demise. Blacks had regained their national citizenship and national citizenship rights and immunities by extracting laws from the national government that restored the Fourteenth and Fifteenth amendments to them, and with teeth in the laws to implement those amendments. Another form of success was that Blacks had forced a redistribution of wealth to them in the form of social programs. A second reason was exhaustion. Blacks had been in struggle for two decades. They were tired and simply could not storm the Bastille anymore. There was also an interest, as a causative factor, in enjoying the achievements of the Movement. These last two reasons, in my view, played a large role in preventing Black Power advocates from being able to take the Black Liberation Movement significantly and progressively beyond its political and civil rights focus. This weakened political position of Black Power and its advocates played into the hands of the White racists, who also weakened these forces by their repressive activities. The White racists were the fifth reason for the demise of the Black Liberation Movement. They had resisted the Movement from the very beginning, determinedly and violently in the South, and with vicious determination in the North as well. But Whites could not stop Blacks in their liberation efforts, and it finally dawned on them that there was not going to be any stoppage until Blacks had achieved their demands. Whites were forced into making the concessions, but the achievements of the Movement played into their hands. They now felt they could draw the line, say that the demands had been met. There was no more reason for struggle. But they did more than think and talk about this. They exerted power through the national and other American governments and through economic and educational institutions, especially those supported by governmental statutes or public support, and also through the print and electronic media, in order to denounce, thwart, or suppress further large demands. But they did more than that: they launched a national restoration of racism in the country, with every intention of strengthening it as much as they could. Blacks, along with their White allies in the struggle, had seriously and successfully assaulted racism. But they had not eliminated it from the minds, personalities, and behavior of most Whites, which meant that this racism would still be exercised in America, in its culture and institutions, and in White-Black social interaction. But Whites did not have it all going for them now. They could not promote racism as they had in the past, which was in any way they had wanted to. They now had to accept the fact, even in the South, that a publicly blatant and violent racism in the country was a thing of the past. It had been exposed publicly, domestically and internationally, for the savagery that it was—to say nothing about the anti-Americanism that it also was. It was now dangerous to engage in that kind of racism in the country, because there were Blacks now who would counter it with the same kind of violence. But any publicly blatant and violent racism in America would be grist for the propaganda mill for the Soviet Union and other communist countries; they would see to it that the world heard about and saw it, especially in countries of people of color. The latter was a deterrent all on its own. People of color who had formerly been colonized people were now living in their own independent countries, were directing national governments and national economies, and were also engaged in international diplomacy and trade. America had to engage in diplomacy and trade with such countries. Blatant and violent racism in the country would greatly complicate and hinder such interactions.

So the blatantly verbal and social and the physically violent forms of White racist behavior had been eclipsed in America and in the continuing American history as mainline forms of racist expression. This was progress in American history and American social life, a movement toward America, what it was and for which it stood. But this movement toward America was not desired by most Whites. It did not come from the conscience, heart, or morality of most Whites. It was a movement toward America and its ideals that was forced upon most Whites by internal and external pressures. And the proof that there was not much altruistic or humanistic motivation for this movement or now, and finally, an understanding of genuine freedom by most Whites in America was the determined and strong effort to keep white supremacy/ebonicism alive and functional in the country. In the late 1960s and thereafter, Blacks and some allied white critics, labeled the new forms of behavior subtle White racism; the focus was on race and not really on racism and on a continued employment of concepts like *prejudice, race, race prejudice, racial discrimination*, or *racial segregation*.

But Blacks and their white allies made the mistake of thinking that this subtle racism was new. It was as old as white supremacy/ebonicism in America, as old as the blatant verbal, social, and physically violent racism in the country, growing up together with the former, being implemented along with it, and helping to reinforce and perpetuate the grosser forms of racism. Whenever white people, from the late seventeenth and early eighteenth centuries on, talked in universal terms about rights, or equality, or opportunities, or progress, or justice, they meant them for Whites only. The concept "we the people" did not include Blacks nor the idea of "preserving American freedom" or the phrase "struggling for liberty." All of these words or phrases were racist code words. They were used by Whites as public signals to each other to encourage the enslavement and subordination of Blacks, to promote the confinement, exclusion, and avoidance of

Blacks, and to deny dignity, courtesies, opportunities, and formal rights to Blacks. All the phrases were also used to hide or cloak the oppression and victimization of Blacks. This traditional subtle racist behavior did not end in the 1950s and 1960s. It was a survivor of the Black Liberation Movement. But since it had also become the dominant form of white supremacist/ebonicistic racist expression in America, Whites, primarily subtle racists now, had to devise new, additional coded words and phrases that would function together with others from the past. Such words and phrases were "conservative," "liberal," "big government," "government spending," "public spending," "welfare," "social programs," "liberal social programs," "balanced budget," "affirmative action," "crime," "law and order," "gun control," "family values," "bussing," "educational vouchers," "fiscal restraint," "Heartland," and a host of others. They were all lines leading to and from the racist thinking and racist psychology of Whites. They were appeals to racism. They were coded words to motivate racists, to organize them, and to get them to implement racism. And all the time this racism was being appealed to and promoted, the word *race*, or *black*, or *Black*, or any reference to Black people or race would not be made. But white racists hearing the words and phrases would know what they meant and what the references were to. It wasn't that Whites were being clever, even if some of them thought that they were. Black people knew what they were doing and said so. But white racists had restored themselves in America with considerable strength, particularly in the major institutions in America. The code words and phrases were an attempt to cover up the continuing racist character of these institutions and the racist perversion of them. About this, Blacks were not fooled. But, again, there was reentrenched White racist power that had to be considered and dealt with—power that could not be totally against protecting the rights and opportunities of Blacks in America or totally against their economic, educational, and social advance because Blacks could bring power to bear on that situation, even Black-White power to bear on it. There was also the outside pressure. But white racists, reentrenched in America, were not going to allow much, if they could help it, in the way of largesse or advancement, and certainly not for the mass of Blacks. The coded racist words and phrases would increase, projected especially by politicians, to mobilize white racists behind this determined, restrictive effort, with the White-owned media, with their own subtle racist orientation, helping to project the coded racist words and phrases and helping politicians to organize and galvanize the White racist resistance. All of this indicated to Black people where most white people still were in their minds and personalities and social behavior and what they still didn't understand about universal human dignity, liberty, equality, opportunities, justice, or a genuine American freedom.

For Black people, Ronald Reagan became the great symbol of the subtle white racist and subtle White racism, which was also stretched to include his two presidential administrations. The electronic and print media got fully behind the Reaganite appeal to subtle White racism and helped Reagan garner the vote for two terms, two Reaganite administrations, in the White House. Ronald Reagan was a "white man's President," and his administrations functioned in the interest of rich and powerful and other white men. Two social scientists described Reagan after his first election to the White House as the "white people's President":

> President Reagan, more than any other President in recent memory, has cultivated an image as the "white people's President." In the 1984 election, Reagan took 74 percent of the white male vote in the South, 68 percent in the West, and 66 percent in the nation as a whole: "Reagan won every category of white males except white Jewish males. . . . He won rich and poor, Catholic and Protestant, young and old, North and South, Yuppie and blue collar. Generally he won them by overwhelming margins."[1]

These writers of *Racial Formation in the United States* would have been more accurate had they said, as I said above, that Reagan was a "white man's President," which their own evidence had confirmed and which Reagan's landslide victory in 1984 confirmed even more. Reagan and his administrations and the millions of Whites in the country, functioning as subtle racists, who followed them and supported them, could not make a distinction between White racist America and America. The two had been pried away from each other by the Black Liberation Movement in the country. But the really strong White racists were incapable of seeing the distinction. Those who were less racist could only see it for a moment. But what they saw, and the way it menaced them, even terrified them, made them want to close down that distinction. These were the White racists who took the lead in constructing and championing subtle racist power and subtle racist coded beliefs and practices. Ronald Reagan became their popular leader, their savior. Saving what? They said he saved America and repeatedly and wildly chanted America's ideals; what they really meant was White racist America. In the mouths of subtle White racists, America and American ideals were coded racist expressions. The coded racist language was part of public discourse and also ordinary, everyday speech in America. This guaranteed making subtle White racism a widespread, everyday phenomenon in America that would menace Black people and America and that would be more difficult for both of them to confront than the blatant White racism.

It was all like a grand conspiracy being conducted in America against Blacks and America, a grand *racist conspiracy.* Some Black intellectuals and Black leaders made the charge about a racist conspiracy against Blacks. Whites, of course, denied the charge. But in truth Whites were the least qualified to assess the extent, the functioning, or the damage of racism to themselves or to Blacks in America. They had been perpetrators of racism, not analysts of it. And they did not want their racism analyzed in any way and fought against its being analyzed, thus keeping themselves in ignorance about their racist thinking, racist psychology, and racist social behavior in the country. I have heard some white people talk about the "innocence" of white racists, because they did not know about themselves as racists or much about the racist behavior they perpetrated. But this was inadequate analysis, with perhaps some lurid motivations as well. White racists were ignorant but could never be considered innocent. Not thinking in anti-human terms and carrying out anti-humane behavior. Not when treating people as Non-Others. There has been a racist conspiracy in America since the late seventeenth and early eighteenth centuries. And subtle White racists continue to carry it out and to keep it as a reality in American history and social life, and it is not, nor does it have to be, a conspiracy in which Whites meet secretly to plot things. Culture and social life create the conspiracy. In the late seventeenth and early eighteenth centuries, White supremacy/ebonicism was embedded deeply in what was then British culture and social life. As culture and social life, most white people had its racist features embedded strongly in their minds, personalities, and social behavior. These embedments in culture and social life and in minds, personalities, and behavior were carried over into American history.

Whites, first in British colonial history, and then in American history, were culturally, socially, intellectually, and psychologically conditioned to respond to Black people in a compulsive, a priori antirational, antihumane, and antisocial manner. They were conditioned to respond these ways whenever and wherever they came in contact with Black people. This behavior reinforced the racist intellectual and psychological traits which, in turn, reinforced the racist social behavior. Blacks observed, analyzed, and were victims of this racist thinking and social behavior, falling victims to it whenever and wherever they interacted with Whites, first in the British colonies and then in America. It was as if Whites were conducting a conspiracy against Blacks, to dominate them, to control them, and to exploit them, which they were doing. Whites invested their racism in the general American society and in the general American civilization to produce a *societal racist conspiracy* and a *civilizational racist conspiracy* that would have American society and American civilization primarily move inhumanely against Blacks. This brought American history in on the conspiracy and created a *historical racist conspiracy* against Blacks. All of these conspiracies were structural formations in America. They were all structures in which Whites participated and through which they acted as racists toward Blacks. The subtle white racists were seeking to carry these various conspiracies and conspiratorial structures into America's future against Blacks and America.

In the midst of this reentrenched White racist power, subtle White racism, and various racist conpiracies, the Black sociologist William Julius Wilson exploded on the scene. In 1978, he published a book entitled *The Declining Significance of Race*.[2] Wilson's purpose for writing the book was to try to keep Black hope and optimism alive and to try to keep Blacks advancing in the country. He felt that could be better done now—and indeed felt that the only way now for Blacks to pursue this objective was for them to move to a new, primary cognitive orientation, from race to social class. In his study, Wilson argued that while there was still considerable racism in American political, educational, religious, family and other societal institutions, racism had declined significantly in America's economic institutions and in the American economy. He asserted that it would be the social class status of Blacks and class factors such as education, cultural and social sophistication, bourgeois values of individual effort, dedication, hard work, sacrifice, and also advanced technical or economic skills, that would determine how successfully Blacks would relate to the contemporary American economy and, therefore, their attainment of success. It was Wilson's contention that if racism ended tomorrow in America, a large number of, if not most, Blacks would not be able to participate effectively or successfully in America's contemporary economy. Those who were not able would join the ranks of what he called the Black "underclass," that vast group among Blacks lacking the education, social development, and technical and economic skills to relate to the American economy in any significant way and which would continue to grow among Blacks.

Needless to say, Wilson's views about the declining significance of race in the American economy and his contention that class status and class factors would determine economic and social outcomes for Blacks was grasped enthusiastically by many Whites: scholars, politicians, and journalists. Wilson's book and viewpoints, a book by and viewpoints of a reputable Black scholar, at the time chairman of the sociology department of the University of Chicago,[3] one of the most prestigious universities in the country, was a godsend to white people who disliked focusing on—and revealing—their racism. Here was a Black scholar, and his book and its analytical concepts and categories could be used to help cover up and strengthen reentrenched White racist power and subtle White racism. Wilson discovered how he and his book were being used to promote cover-up, deception, and racism—the subtle racism of which he was fully knowledgeable and on which he himself had written. Whites who praised him and his book said that this Black scholar had said that racism was over in America, that it was no longer a serious factor in American life, that America was a color-blind society, that Blacks were not to have preferential or special treatment, and that Blacks would have to acquire the same educational and technical and economic skills as Whites and be just as meritorious as they to be economically and socially successful in America. Wilson had not said that White racism against Blacks was over in America. This racism still functioned strongly in America, in a subtle form, save in economic institutions and the American economy, where blatant racism had disappeared and where the subtle racism was not as extensive as in other areas of American life. Thus, he had not said that America was "color-blind." He had argued that Black middle-class people already exhibited the same cultural, social, and economic prerequisites to compete in the contemporary American economy and to be successful. But he had also argued that the Black "underclass" needed some special help to rise from that class and to succeed in America. But Wilson's praisers had not been interested in these arguments, just their own, that they had invested in his book—exhibiting typical White racist behavior of projecting and accepting fantasy, instead of reality.

These were all things that Black scholars other than Wilson saw, as well as other Black intellectuals and Black political elements. A number of Black scholars chastised Wilson themselves for what they thought were wrong or "premature" conclusions, such as the wrong view that racism had significantly declined in the American economy, his "premature" view about the crystallization and clear-cut differentiation of social classes among Blacks, and, thus, the "premature" conclusion about the great importance of class determinants in Black life. Some Black scholars plunged into research to check out Wilson's interpretations and conclusions about what was happening socially among Blacks and his argument about the serious diminution of racism in American economic institutions and in the American economy. Sociologist Sharon Collins plunged into this kind of research and produced some results. She acknowledged that a Black middle class existed in America, that it was getting larger, and that the situation was leading to class differentiation in the Black community. But she also argued that racism still strongly affected Black employment opportunities, even the kind of work Blacks did. She noted that in governmental institutions and economic corporations, Blacks typically worked at "Black jobs" such as jobs in the criminal justice area in governmental institutions and in public relations or community relations jobs in corporate economic institutions, relating to and serving, in either job capacity, Black clienteles and Black clienteles only.[4] Bart Landry argued in his book, *The New Black Middle Class*,[5] published a decade after Wilson's study, that the Black middle class was subjected to what I call white supremacy/ebonicism in the American economic system. And journalist Ellis Cose recorded the Black middle-class's resentment of the racism they were subjected to daily in economic corporations in his book *The Rage of a Privileged Class*,[6] published in the early 1990s.

What Black scholars had to say in criticism of Wilson forced him to look more closely at his own views, even to alter or pare down some of his initial remarks. But Wilson's Black critics would not have any impact on the Whites who praised Wilson, especially since he stuck to his guns about the role of social class and social class factors as the required new cognition for Blacks and their importance for future Black economic and social success in America. Such people also turned a deaf ear because they heard other Black voices that were essentially in support of Wilson and whose understandings of things and language usage were replicas of their own. These people, scholars, journalists, or economic elements, called themselves, and were called by Whites, conservatives.

I want to say a few things about the Black conservatives, but there is an observation I wish to make first about Black progress and how it has been achieved in America. I make these remarks to disclose a chunk of American historical reality, but also as something that stands as a check on anyone, Black or white, who suggests that Black progress is to be achieved simply by doing what other people in America have done to make progress, that is, what white people have done. This makes my remarks something I wish to proffer specifically to Black conservatives.

Wilson made the point in his book, and it remains his position, that structural changes in the American economy, organizational, scientific, technological, productive, and distributive, presently exclude millions of Blacks from participating adequately or sucessfully in the American economy and that this situation will get worse unless such Blacks acquire the means, class means, to do so. There have been many structural changes in the American economy over the history of the country. These changes took place when most Blacks were slaves, but this did not affect their employment in the country. What affected their employment was that there were white people who depended on and needed their labor. This was true in the late nineteenth century, when the economic corporation became the main organizational, productive, and commercial unit in the American economy, which was abetted by scientific and technological innovations. Most Black people lived in the South and worked there as farmers or agricultural laborers, millions as new slaves. Again Blacks worked at virtually full employment. Contemporary developments in the American economy did not determine whether or not Blacks were employed. What determined it was that there were white people who were dependent upon and needed Black labor. During the First World War, Blacks worked in the war industries of the North because their labor was needed. It took some strong protest to open up the war industries to Blacks during the Second World War, but there was also a need for Black labor as well, as white men were taken from the country to go to war. The structural changes of the economy during the time of the First World War, then during the Second World War, did not keep Blacks from work. Dependency on Black labor determined employment, even if teaching Blacks skills on the job to enable them to work was necessary.

And then there is another way to look at Black economic progress in America, as well as other forms of political, educational, and social progress, that also involved a dependency on Blacks as an important element in Blacks' attaining various kinds of progress. It can be argued that Blacks have made their greatest advances in America when white people have fallen out with each other, and Blacks were drawn in as vital, needed participants. In the late eighteenth century, white British and white developing Americans went to war. This resulted in the abolition of the African slave trade to the northern part of the new America and the institution of a program of gradual abolition of slavery in the region. Five thousand Blacks ultimately fought in the war and helped the developing Americans defeat the British. Many were slaves, and those who were slaves were released from bondage and primarily went North to try to make an independent and better life for themselves. This period, which carried into the early nineteenth century, was a time when a northern Black community was more fully constructed in America.

In the 1860s, northern and southern Whites fell out with each other and went to war with each other. Blacks ultimately joined in the war as participants, hundreds of thousands strong. The result was the abolition of slavery, amendments and laws that gave and guaranteed Blacks citizenship, citizenship rights, and immunities. Former slaves also made efforts to buy land and to establish educational institutions. Both efforts were aided by Whites. And a big achievement and a great gain for Blacks, again aided by Whites, was laying the foundation for the historic Black colleges and universities in the South that would become the primary producers of Black college and university graduates or, to say it another way, Black professionals in America.

In 1914, white people fell out again. This time it was white people in Europe falling out with one another and going to war. America became a supplier for the war, but it faced a labor shortage when European immigrants were no longer able to come to the country. Maintaining its position as supplier and maintaining an interest in making enormous profits from the war, northern industry, the primary source for European war supplies from the country, needed labor. It drew on Blacks in the North and drew up hundreds of thousands of Blacks from the South to work in the war industries. This meant hundreds of thousands of Blacks with higher wages, larger incomes, more spending power. This led to a greater development of Black businesses, a higher standard of living for Blacks, more educated Blacks, and more Black professionals. The depression of the 1930s diminished many of these gains. But another White fallout and another war in the 1940s restored them, as northern Blacks and Blacks from the South worked in northern war industries with southern Blacks also working in newly created war production southern industries. The results for Blacks, North and South, were economic, educational, social, and professional gains. In the 1950s and 1960s, there was a falling out between northern Whites and southern Whites, which Blacks themselves instigated through their Liberation Movement in the country. Whites became dependent upon Blacks to keep the struggle from destroying the United States. Martin Luther King, Jr., found a way to produce change without provoking massive violence from Whites; his method of nonviolent direct action prevented the country from plunging into self-destruction and permitted it to regenerate and change itself and to keep on reaching for its true self. This brought, and rightly and justly so, the honor of a national holiday for Martin Luther King, Jr. America bestowed the honor proudly. White racist America loathed it and recoiled against it.

The dependency of Whites and America on the intelligence and restraint of Blacks in struggle and their love for and loyalty to America helped to squeeze the concessions from Whites: laws, economic gains, educational gains, health care gains, social gains, such as the expanded growth of educated Blacks, the expanded growth of the Black middle class, and the expanded growth of Black professionals, including Black professionals in governmental administration. The conflict between the United States and the Soviet Union, with propaganda on the side of the Soviet Union, and the watchful eyes of people of color on the planet, who viewed America through their ambassadors, their representatives at the United Nations, and on television, acted as pressures on White racists and White racist America to treat Blacks better and to help them make some cultural and social progress.

Clearly the history of Black people shows that the progress of Blacks, in all areas of their life in America, has depended primarily on *political factors*, as a consequence of political factors external to them but which they participated in for benefit. Or it came as a consequence of their own direct political behavior to make progress of all kinds in the country. This situation has not changed. William Wilson recognizes this, at least partially. He has always been and remains a strong advocate of what he calls the Black "underclass' " right to receive extensive national government help to become participants in the contemporary American economy and to get out of the underclass and into the Black middle class. In 1987 he spoke directly to these matters in his book entitled *The Truly Disadvantaged.*[7] His thesis was that government aid to the Black underclass should not be based on racial criteria, that is, should not be "race specific," but should be part of a broad government effort to help all truly disadvantaged and needy people in America.

Getting away from race—or staying away from it, as it were—keeps Wilson's white admirers listening to him, but they still listen less to him than to their own emendations of what he says. The stay-away-from-race approach still keeps his Black conservative support, as does Wilson's continuing talk about social class among Blacks and class factors as determinants of employment or occupational opportunities, and social advancement. A number of Black conservatives reject his idea of government aid, even to what he calls, and even that they call, the Black underclass, since most of these individuals are against a social role, or at least an extensive social role, for government in American society. Their focus is on the individual, the Black individual, and what the Black individual can do for him or herself, on his or her own initiative. The conservatives outdo white people in talking about the individual. But a lot of white people love it, and particularly the subtle White racists. They love as well the Black conservative attack against extensive government aid to Blacks and the Black conservative attack on what both call Black liberal leadership that advocates extensive government aid. Subtle white racists have made Black conservatives their favorite Blacks and give them extensive access to the media to air their views. It's the traditional White racist behavior of exploiting Blacks for White gain. Subtle White racists hide behind Black conservatives, as they hide behind phrases such as *structural changes in the economy*, and the notion of *class status, class factors*, and *individual efforts* as social determinants, which are all, for these people, coded racist phrases, that promote subtle White racism.

Black conservatives are aware of this charge of aiding the entrenchment and functioning of subtle White racism. But they are not, as a rule, fazed by it, so strongly do they believe in their position and so blinded are they by it as a rule. They are blinded by the myth of individualism in America that greatly affects their thinking about individualism as a social method of advance. Sociologist Barry Barnes has written about the American individualism myth:

> Individualist theorists seem perfectly willing to concede that their postulates and actual human behavior diverge. They tend to justify individualism not by challenging the evidence that calls it into question but in other ways. One is to . . . suggest that the "rationality" defined by the postulates represents how individuals "ought" to behave, so that the postulates provide the basis for a normative not a descriptive social theory. Another way is to insist that useful models can be constructed from the postulates; since the models "work," there is, so it is said, no need to worry about the truth or falsity of the postulates. Yet another way is to find virtue in the models even when they fail to "work." . . . Indifference to the truth or falsity of theoretical assumptions is widespread in the social sciences and defended by sociologists of many different inclinations.[8]

The Black conservatives, a number of whom are sociologists, defend the individualism myth, meaning that they romanticize and fantasize about it and its social efficacy. As they continue to do so, they ignore or downplay the reality of the political factors that fundamentally determine Black economic and social success in America. Moreover, they have not answered satisfactorily and, indeed, have not raised the question as to why what they call class factors and class determinants have to be associated exclusively with an individual or social class. The same determinants, such as education, cultural and social sophistication, and the bourgeois values of individual effort, dedication, hard work, sacrifice, and advanced technical and economic skills could also be embraced by an ethnic group and individuals of that group in the same way that such factors can apply to a gender group and members of that group and a social class and individuals of that class. Black people are an ethnic group in America. But this is something that most Black conservatives do not know. Even if it were made clear to them, most of them would reject this reality, because they do not like ethnic groups or organic collectivities. Jews, Italians, Irish, Greeks, and Poles put a priority on themselves as individuals, but many in each group still make space in their lives for their ethnic ancestry, ethnic status, and ethnic identity. But Black conservatives see an essential incompatibility between an individual and group status and an individual identity and a group identity. One of these Black conservatives is Shelby Steele, who wrote in his book *The Content of Our Character*, which the publishers of the book touted as "A New Vision of Race in America":

> I believe this impulse causes our most serious strategic mistake: to put the responsibility for our racial development more in the hands of the collective than in the hands of the individuals who compose it. . . . But while civil rights bills can be won this way, only the individual can achieve in school, master a salable skill, open a business, and become an accountant or an engineer. Despite our collective oppression, opportunities for development can finally be exploited only by individuals.[9]

If this is supposed to be a new vision, it is not. The slave who became a hired-out laborer for economic gain for himself and his master was the individual slave taking advantage of an opportunity, a Black individual making progress under slavery, under oppression. Individual Blacks by the thousands in American and Black history have made individual advancement under oppression, despite oppression. This is a strong tradition among Blacks, not something new. It is something old, and it continues. Pitted against this tradition and reality of individual effort and advancement is the reality of millions of Blacks in the past and today not making it in America and who will not make it as individuals in the future in the country. There are reasons for that: the continuing white supremacy/ebonicism in the country that continues to say this country belongs to white people, particularly white men, and that Black people, at least most Black people, are to be kept down and are to be locked out of significant benefits.

Steele, as well as other Black conservatives, seem to think there is an incompatibility or necessary difference between group values and individual values. Or perhaps they suggest something wrong or impossible in a group preparing, inspiring, or helping individual members achieve. Group pride can be a source of individual pride and a source of motivation and success. And there are the hard historical reality and the hard historical fact that it has taken Blacks, acting as a group, to open up opportunities for large numbers of Black individuals in America, including Black conservatives. Realistically, what are the chances of many individual Blacks advancing when white racists feel that the Black group is weak and no threat and cannot help many Black individuals advance? What would be the chance of many Black individuals advancing if the Black group were strong, perceived as such, and ready to defend and push individual Black efforts in American society?

One last criticism of Black conservatives and their narrow either-or and simplistically construed individualist ideology. American society is composed of vast centralized political, economic, and social institutions. These institutions are dominated and controlled by white people, particularly by white men. It has been primarily white men who have dominated, controlled, and exploited Black people in America. This was not just done on an individual basis. It was also done on a group basis, the group being the white male gender group. Black conservatives seldom talk about white men and their domination, control, and exploitation of America or of Black people. White men, especially those who fall into the cateory of rich and powerful or the category of the dominant element, have never been against the national or state governments giving them help to do what they want to do in America, including what they have wanted to do to Black people. Black conservatives seldom say anything about these matters and seem consciously to avoid doing so; but they readily and consciously and often bitterly pounce on Black intellectuals or Black leaders who think American governments, the governments of Black people, should help them.

Invariably and regularly Black conservatives condemn the United States governments for providing public assistance, popularly known as *welfare*—White racist thinking and political behavior have it made "welfare" in the public imagination—to Black people. Whites seldom say *public assistance* and use the racist phrase *welfare*, seldom mentioning that most people on "welfare" in America are white women and children and white indigent. Proportionately, compared to Whites, more Blacks receive public assistance. But there are important reasons that this is so. This is where powerful white men want most Black people to be, functioning out of that racist/slave history and mentality that conceives of Blacks under domination and control, living on plantations or in ghettoes, or incarcerated in jails and prisons.

"Welfare" (or public assistance) is a primary means to segregate and to continue segregating Black people in ghettoes in the United States. "Welfare" is a substitution for educating masses of Black people or training them for skilled work or good jobs and also functions simultaneously to keep masses of Black people out of the job market as educated and/or as skilled labor and instead holds them in place as a massive source of cheap labor. Without the educational, financial, or occupational means, masses of Blacks have to stay put in ghettoes. Many will engage in crime and many will be incarcerated.

People seem not to realize, and even Black people often forget it, that "welfare" programs are designed primarily by white men functioning as elected or appointed public officials, as consultants, or as staff personnel, that they primarily legislate the programs, and that white men are heavily involved in administering the programs as government officials, administrators, or as staff. White women are also heavily involved in the administration of "welfare," nationally and at the state and local level. When "welfare" fails, as the American public is told periodically (and also periodically that it needs to be "reformed"), the American people, including Black Americans, do not understand this to mean that this pronounced failure is primarily that of white men, those white men who primarily designed, legislated, and financed the programs or services. The "reform" in question is nothing more than the same white men, deceptively projecting a public posture of progressiveness or responsibility, to cover up what has to be their own failure of conception and capability of implementation. And they get other white people, even some Black people, namely, Black conservatives, to engage in these deceptions by talking about the failure of "welfare" and blaming Blacks for the failure when Blacks (and other recipients of "welfare") have virtually no say in or control over programs or services provided them.

But the "failure" of "welfare" is a deception in another, equally insidious way. "Welfare" has never failed in America. It has always succeeded for what it has always been designed and legislated and intended to accomplish: making upper-class white men rich or richer, white middle-class people more affluent, and maintaining the mass of Black people and other poor people at the subsistance level, to keep them out of the skilled-labor, high-paying job market as vast sources of cheap labor and also as political scapegoats.

As expected, white racists and White racist America have made Black men, but particularly Black women and Black children the primary scapegoats with respect to "welfare." As K. Sue Jewell has written:

> The American public is regularly exposed to images of African American women as welfare recipients, procreating large numbers of children without the benefit of fathers who are willing and able to care for their offspring. Implicit in these messages is the message that through their welfare dependence, African American women are deriving benefits from tax dollars while others (white others) are being deprived of societal resources. It is held by those who construct and control the proliferation of cultural images that most members of society are more entitled to the resources they are being denied than are African American women and their children. Using cultural images, those in power have constructed the image of welfare as being primarily an institutional support system for African American females, and their charges.[10]

Jewell makes a good argument, but she also weakens it. The above are not just cultural images; they are racist images, white supremacist/ebonicistic. This shows through clearly when it is remembered that most people on "welfare" are white women, children, and white indigent, and yet they are not implicated in the media "welfare" images. And the people propagating these images are not just "those in power," but white racists in power, mainly white male racists. The latter engage in this racism and project these racist images to cover up or distract people from some palpable realities about "welfare" provision in America.

"Welfare" or public assistance, whichever of these it is called, is a government subsidy program, primarily for upper- and middle-class white men, but also for many middle-class white women. When Blacks, for instance, receive "welfare" payments, they cannot keep the money or save any of it. They have to spend it. With whom do they spend it? Primarily with upper- and middle-class white men and some white women of these classes. Upper-class white men are primarily the owners or top-level managers of the national chain food stores, national chain clothing stores, or the national chain pharmacies where Blacks spend portions of their "welfare" checks. Food stamps is a big subsidy of American agriculture, particularly the large agribusinesses, which are owned primarily by upper-class white men. They also are the ones who primarily own the packing, the packaging, and the distributing businesses of agricultural produce but also the packaging and distributing businesses of other products that Black and other people on "welfare" buy. Upper- and middle-class white men especially, own the tenements, the apartment buildings, or the houses that Blacks and others on "welfare" pay rent to live in. Many white middle-class men and women provide professional services to Blacks and others on "welfare." The salaries and wages of the white people who administer "welfare" programs or investigate their implementation are paid out of "welfare" budgets. But inasmuch as there are a number of Black people involved in administering "welfare" programs at the national, state, and local level, this kind of public spending—"welfare" spending—is a subsidy for them, too, and is also a subsidy for Black professionals who provide Black "welfare" recipients with professional services. Black property owners benefit from "welfare." "Welfare" spending and "welfare" programs and services have played a large role in helping to build and expand the Black middle class in America.

As can be seen, many people in America have a stake in "welfare." They get rich or richer from it, gain wealth and affluence from it, or gain wealth, affluence, and elevated social status from it. And there are the scores of millions, with many of the millions of Black people, who are kept alive with it, consciously and purposely at the maintenance level. But the white male rich of America, from slaveholder to industrialist and businessman, have understood clearly that poor people can make other people rich or richer by their labor and by their dimes, nickels, and pennies. A cut in "welfare" payments in the form of cash benefits or a cut in the financing of "welfare" programs or services does not necessarily represent a cut in government or public spending. What it usually means, as a conscious, intended activity, is a shifting or transference of the *cut* monies to other parts of the national, state, or local budgets and the routing of this money in these ways, principally to upper-class white men and other white people. Robert Woodson is a Black conservative who knows how the "welfare system" works in America and how, functioning in a racist-inundated manner, it works mainly for rich and powerful, affluent white people. But he has yet (to my knowledge) fully to clarify to Black conservatives, other Blacks, and other people in America what he knows. When seen on television, usually in some debate setting, he constantly finds himself fending off his Black or white liberal opposition. Only a smattering of his knowledge about the "welfare system" comes through. But his understanding about how government should relate to Blacks or help them in America seems to have the same weaknesses and limitations found among other Black conservatives. Black economist Walter Williams is another Black conservative who knows how the "welfare system" works in America and how it mainly benefits upper- and middle-class White men. But he is also like Woodson in having a limited vision of America's governments helping Black citizens and helping them to advance.

Back to the vast centralized institutions in America. Another way of looking at them is to see them as vast centralized structures. They are massive structures in which and through which rich and powerful white men and other white men, and many white women as well, function. Most of these white people are racists of some degree, subtle racists of some degree now. But they invest the racism that is in them and maintain it in the institutions in which they function, making them function strongly or considerably in a racist manner and making and maintaining these institutions strongly or considerably racist, or perverted structures. What chance does an individual Black person have going up against a vast, centralized, essentially racist institution? What chances do a number of individual Black people have, acting alone and separately, to do this? These same centralized institutions are generally pro–white individual and function in behalf of individual Whites, especially individual white men. Against vast, centralized, racist-inundated institutions, Blacks have to possess and implement effective collective Black Power, meaning effective Black ethnic community power. This is the hope for the millions of Black people who have not made it in America, whose chances of making it dim sharply as time goes on; they are also the means to help the Blacks who have advanced to hold onto—at least that—their gains. These are among the number of things that Black conservatives, with their conservative and their one-dimensional thinking, cannot see. They do not see the danger now lurking for Blacks (and other poor— and even many middle-class—people in America) now that the Soviet Union no longer exists. The corporate capitalists and the corporate economic system in America no longer have to face a Soviet or general communist threat. Corporate capitalists as well as politicians, journalists, and academics also see this as the triumph and vindication of American corporate capitalism and this system generally in the world. Robert Helibroner recently wrote, "It is likely that capitalism will be the principal form of socioeconomic organization during the twenty-first century, at least for the advanced nations, because no blueprint exists for a viable successor."[11] This is the economic system that thinks of growth in terms of production, investment, big dividends, and high unemployment. This trend will continue into the twenty-first century, and with the continued expansion and use of technology for economic production and the continued severe reduction of human labor for production unemployment will not only be constantly high but will be held in a continuous spiraling pattern. It was once remarked by sociologist Sidney Wilhelm, that many, many, Blacks were no longer needed for the American economy. He made this observation in a provocative book in 1970 entitled *Who Needs the Negro?*[12] Years later William Julius Wilson augmented that thought and concern. But the thought and concern have to be expanded; the question today is bigger, given the way the white men who own or manage the economic corporations (95 percent of the top-level management positions) and the way they make the corporate economy function: *who needs millions of Americans?* But if the choice were between utilizing white or Black people for America's future corporate capitalistic activities and the American corporate economy, it is clear who the white men who own or manage these structures—along with their political, journalistic, and academic allies—would choose.

That is only one potential big future worry for Blacks and millions of other Americans. The corporate capitalists in America and Europe and elsewhere in the world want all the public money they can get, that is, all the public taxes or all the taxpayers' money they can get. They want it to augment their stocks and dividends and high salaries, without their initially producing or selling anything. They also want it to increase their investment capabilities, their take-over ability, their corporate geographical expansion, and their corporate economic production and sales. They have always been greedy about this. During the Reagan and George Bush years, they showed how much. But the gateway to greater greed is open. There is no longer a Soviet or communist, or even a strong socialist threat—forces like these—to inhibit greed and to force upon the economic, political, and intellectual elements that combine to make corporate economic institutions and the corporate economy function the way they do great social concerns and specifically a great concern for the economic and social future of scores of millions of Americans. The public money that the American corporate capitalists and their political and intellectual allies are strongly, if not primarily after is the money that finances social programs or social services—specifically, the money that goes to millions of Blacks and other poor people in America who have no political means to protect themselves or to save themselves. But whatever money is taken from social spending and public assistance programs and shifted to the corporate capitalists and their institutions will be money also taken from the white and other middle-class people who administer public assistance programs or provide social services, as well as the small businesses that rely for their existence on the spending that "welfare" recipients do with them. The current national "welfare reform," in my view, is a signal to the American people that the corporate capitalists and their political and intellectual allies are marking Americans and the American future for great fleecing and misery. Racism, white supremacy/ebonicism especially, but other racisms as well, will be strong contributors to, and guides of, this behavior. And the same racisms of the millions of affected white people will prevent them from seeing, or seeing clearly, or understanding the behavior going on and what it really means. For Blacks it will be the same old rule-of-thumb story with respect to the American economy: that when it hurts white people, it devastates them. But in reality, many Americans are going to be devasted in the future if there are no significant changes in how American society and the American economy function. Sociologist John Walton refers clearly to this situation:

> In the not-distant past, agriculture employed nearly half the population of the developed societies. Today the United States can feed itself and a good many more through the efforts of 3 percent of the population. More important, where industry once grew in a process that steadily incorporated a larger labor force, it now advances with labor-saving technology. The new computer technology requires less labor for its production. The central importance of these facts is that previously the distributional mechanisms of the state and economy were connected directly to the job. That is, the mechanisms that raised money for social programs such as Social Security and unemployment insurance and distributed those benefits according to eligibility

criteria were based on the condition of long-term, steady, well-paid jobs throughout the economy.

As industry and profits expanded and concentrated, an improved standard of living *did* trickle down to the general population in the developed countries. State guarantees of social welfare were linked directly to employment or indirectly to the programs maintained by working people and by employers on a per-capita worker basis. Now, however, with a sharp decline in the number of jobs that are needed in the productive segments of the economy, the linchpin of the distributional mechanism falls out. In its absence, the only way to provide for the well-being of increasing numbers of people is through direct transfer payments, or what has been called welfare—a system that was never designed for large numbers and indeed was to be supported by a fully employed work force.

The final and noteworthy conclusion is that the welfare state, as it has been conceived, will not work in our technological future.[13]

Now some questions are appropos. Who owns and/or controls the banks, insurance companies, and other financial institutions that finance America's corporate economy? Black people? Who negotiates, directs, and controls America's foreign trade, which affects the American economy and American employment? Black people? Who owns and controls America's corporate capitalistic institutions? Black people? Who owns, dominates, and controls America's corporate capitalist economy? Black people? Who develops and uses the continually advancing technology for economic production in America? Black people? Who owns and controls this technology that dispenses with American people's labor? Black people? Who supports and facilitates this behavior with laws and economic policies and upholds these things in court rulings? Black people? Who owns and/or controls the media that bombards Americans with the "just" decisions and actions of the corporate capitalists and corporate economic institutions? Black people? Who can offer jobs to millions of Americans? Who can take jobs from millions of them? Black people? Who can provide hundreds of thousands of jobs for people all around the world and take jobs from hundreds of thousands of Americans? Black people? Who can provide annual incomes for millions of Americans, or take them away, or slash such incomes and the standard of living that goes with them? Black people? Who will force upon the country in the future "welfare" or public assistance help for millions of Americans or a life of poverty and misery for millions? Black people?

White racists, blatant or subtle, will doubtlessly put the responsibility for this possible negative future behavior, which will grossly negatively affect the lives of scores of millions of Americans, on Black people. They will, doubtlessly, blame Black people and other people of color in America whom racists and other Whites refer to as "minorities" or "racial minorities"—the people who will be hurt the most by this kind of grossly negative behavior. But why would white racists blame such people? Why would they not be joining with them to protect and advance futures together in America? After all, they're being hurt by the same people. Why not? Because their racism will not let them. It will not let their minds or personalities function in the necessary ways to perceive or understand these realities. Their racist-afflicted minds and personalities, their scapegoat thinking and psychological compulsions, and their coiled emotions will tell them to ignore the evidence, ignore the facts, ignore the obvious, to make the illogical and impossible logical and possible—to "cling to a fascinating delusion while rejecting a palatable reality" and then show outrage and self-righteous indignation. Doubtlessly, one will hear often in the future the kind of comment that can be heard often right now, while the reality of the future is being seeded and developed to go later into full operation: "I'm sick of the whole . . . mess. . . . I don't think I'm a racist. But they've gone too far with this thing. Blacks are getting privileges I can't get, my kids can't get. They get into schools with lower grades than whites. They get jobs with lower qualifications than whites. This is not equal opportunity. I'm fed up and so is everyone I talk to." These remarks, made by an outraged white man, were quoted in Patricia J. Williams's book, *The Rooster's Egg*.[14] Look at what this man—and others like him—were fed up with. See also what they were not only not fed up with, but what they were not capable, because of the racism they deny they posses and exhibit, of perceiving or giving any thought to—namely, the white men who play around with and disorganize, limit, or even crush their lives and the lives of their families.

The white racists of the future, as in the past and present, will blame Blacks especially for their economic or social deprivations or dispossessions, and will not blame or hold responsible the only people who have the power, wealth, and inclination to make their lives so ardous and diminished (other than what their own limitations contribute to)—and that is rich and/or powerful white men in the economy and government and their white male academic and journalistic allies. Racists, as they have done in the past, as they presently do and will do in the future, let these elements not only get off the hook for what they do, but let them—because of their self-deceived and crippled and misdirected thought and energy—manipulate the American scene and the people in it in their own behalf—and that means to their great benefit. They will do this with the same ease, fervor, and callousness in the future in America unless some significant changes in perception, understanding, explanation, and political behavior occur in this country, especially on the part of white people.

Back to the matter of Black people and considerations of how they should relate to Black conservatives. In my view, these are not people (as a rule) whom Black people can look to either for analyses or speculations similar to those made above, for vigilance on their behalf, or for suggestions or proposals for emergency or long-term help. They cannot look to Black conservatives for their salvation or future in America, not to people who are overbearing elitest and who shirk social responsibility to Blacks in the guise of advocating an individualist method of social advance. Bluntly, Blacks cannot afford, and it would be foolish and irresponsible on their part to do so, to let Black conservatives (with only a few exceptions) function as their eyes, ears, and guides to thought and action in America. It would overwhelmingly be like viewing themselves through the thoughts and eyes, as well as following the guidance of, subtle white racists and subtle White racist America and relying upon these elements for help in the country. Blatant White racist America was an enormous disaster for Black people. Subtle White racist America can fall on Blacks that way, too, if it goes unresisted or is met with only half-hearted resistance and inadequate thinking and corrective proposals and actions.

8.

Racism and the Question of Intelligence I

The subtle White racists, like the blatant and subtle white racists before them, and like the blatant white racists who still hang on in America, centralize their racism, beliefs, and practice, in one particular racist belief: that white people are naturally cerebrally, or naturally *intellectually* superior to black people and Black people. In their racist orientation, this intellectual disparity between white people and black people is permanent and cannot be appreciably altered by history, culture, or social life, that is, generally, by environment. It is this very low level of natural cerebral endowment that puts black people or Black people down to the level of animal or creature, down to the level of nonhuman or subhuman, or Non-Other. As Abraham Lincoln said to a white audience during one of his debates with Stephen Douglas and as previously quoted: "In pointing out that more has been given you, you cannot be justified in taking away the little which has been given him. . . . If God gave him but little, that little let him enjoy."

Here Lincoln was expressing a general White racist belief, an ebonicistic racist belief, that God was responsible for the low-level natural cerebral endowment of Black people. White people had nothing to do with this; the suppressive environments that white people kept

Black people in, the oppressive slave environment and the oppressive racist environment, had nothing to do with the cerebral endowment or capability of Black people. The fact that white slaveholders in the South made it illegal to teach Black slaves to read and write, to say nothing about otherwise educating them, and for more than two centuries, had nothing to do with the cerebral situation of Black people. The fact that southern Whites segregated Black people in inferior schools, in a very severe manner, for about eighty years, between the 1880s and 1960s, and still segregate many Blacks in the region in very inferior schools has nothing, in the minds of southern Whites or northern Whites, to do with the situation of the intellectual endowment or capability of Black people. The fact that so many white teachers in northern schools assume that Black children are incapable of thinking and learning and do not make a great effort to teach them or put them in classes or give them curricula that will not seriously stimulate their brains, has nothing to do with the situation. White people are guiltless, innocent, and nonresponsible. What white people actually engaged in, throughout all these years, throughout centuries in America, with respect to Blacks, were crimes against Black humanity. Crimes against the Black mind, the Black psychology, the Black being. But, of course, throughout the centuries, Whites, functioning as racists, did not regard their behavior as being criminal or as having, on a continuous basis, committed crimes against Black people and their humanity. They said Black people were criminals and that they committed crimes. They specifically argued that a low-level cerebral capacity made them criminal by nature and prone to commit crime. They pointed to laws that Black people violated and arrested and prosecuted them as criminals for violating formal laws. But Whites, to keep from thinking of themselves as criminals, as committing crimes against Black humanity and Black people, passed laws, or enforced customs that legalized or authorized—what Black people would describe as their immoral thoughts and lawless and criminal social and physical behavior—against them. Which group, Blacks or Whites, had the intelligent view of this situation? Which group was showing intellectual paralysis or inadequacy?

In the early 1900s, white people hit upon a new way to "prove" that Black people were cerebrally inferior to them. They always had to have this understanding, which gave them the greatest assurance about who they were and who Black people were and why they were on top in American society and why Black people were on the bottom. Why they were entitled to and had opportunities and why Black people were not and should not have any, or at least, not many—economically, socially, or culturally. This new, magical, and wonderful device was the *intelligence test*. It was a godsend because, as white racists told themselves, it was scientific. At last scientific proof could be offered that Blacks were cerebrally inferior to Whites. Of course, this also involved a lapse of memory. There had been assumed scientific explanations in the past to account for the alleged cerebral differences between white people and black people. In the eighteenth century, the century of the European Enlightenment, which also penetrated America, scientists and other intellectuals argued that the environment accounted for such differences. The European and American environments were the best environments in the world, which was why white people had and exhibited the greater intelligence and the greater cultural capabilities: "The prevailing Enlightenment view of a hierarchy of all Creation with Europeans on the highest rung, and with differences the product not of inherent characteristics but of environment, dominated thinking in England and the United States in the eighteenth century. All peoples were capable of change and improvement."[1] This was the kind of thinking that some intellectuals did on both sides of the Atlantic (although in both cases failing consciously to think about—which would have been rending thought—the black, Black, and red people who lived in the same geographical environment as they and other Whites. This suggests that racist thinking and racist assumptions were part of this environmental explanation, even though not articulated or consciously understood, standing as a predicate of it).

Masses of white people in the British colonies, contemplating or interacting with Blacks, and with a great fear of blackness (the racial characteristics of Blacks) did not have the Enlightenment environmental viewpoint and regarded differences between themselves and Blacks to be related to biology or race, or, to say it differently, to *inherent* qualities. There were intellectuals in the colonies who had this view, too; they, in fact, vigorously rejected the Enlightenment's scientific explanation that the environment was the deciding factor. They had what they regarded as their own scientific view of the situation. It was actually no different from the common or popular view, but it had a name, which was not used by the mass of Whites in the British colonies, who would not have likely heard of it. Its use by intellectuals separated them from the mass of Whites and, thus, strengthened their own conviction that their view of things was a scientific view. The word was *polygenesis* or *polygenetic*, referring to the inherent inequalities of physical and intellectual attributes between races, particularly the white and black races.

It was difficult for the polygenesis explanation to make headway among intellectuals in Europe or North America in the eighteenth century because of the extensive acceptance of the environmental explanation among intellectuals in both places and, also in both places, the wider acceptance of the monogenesis explanation for humanity. This was fundamentally the Christian theological explanation (but also a part of Enlightenment thought), which said that there was only one human species and that there was a unity of humankind. This view was strong in the British colonies, but it was undergoing erosion. As they continued to interact with Indians and Blacks, whom they regarded as being both savages or creatures and treated that way, Whites in the colonies continuously kicked against the religious doctrine that talked of a single human species and the unity of humankind. Whites wanted conceptual as well as physical and social separation from Blacks and Indians. This created a space for the polygenesis doctrine to exist, even if it could not thrive at the time. But this racist need of Whites led to another explanation for inherent differences between Whites and Blacks (as well as between Whites and Indians). This explanation was theological, but it was a peculiar theology. There were white clergymen in the British colonies and in Western Europe who argued that God had engaged in two acts of human creation, not one—one act to create the white race and white people, to endow them with the superior inherent qualities they had, and another act to create the black race and black people to endow them with the inferior inherent qualities that they had. Support for this argument could not be found in Scriptures, but that did not bother white clergy and other Whites who believed and accepted it as true. They made it up, a purely fanciful belief, but it worked for them. It gave them what they regarded as knowledge and truth about themselves and other Whites and Blacks. But, as one might ask, was this intelligent thinking? Claiming a greater intellectual capability, why would some Whites produce a view that was so unintelligent and even nonsensical? Did racism that is, white supremacy/ebonicism have something to do with this? Did it suppress their intellectual capability, rather than augment it? White people were not daunted by this kind of unintelligent, irrational thinking. Their supposed greater intellectual ability could not even help them understand that their thinking was unintelligent, as well as irrational. Their supposed greater intellectual ability did not help them understand that the white supremacist/ebonicistic racist beliefs they were evolving in the eighteenth century, which they would greatly expand on in the nineteenth century, were unintelligent and irrational. These racist beliefs were not just fanciful and irrational, they were also abstract. But the supposed greater intelligence of Whites did not help them understand that abstract thinking was not ipso facto or necessarily intelligent thinking and, indeed, could be pure unintelligent thinking. Racist fantasies did not equal knowledge and understanding. They equalled nonknowledge and nonunderstanding. *What the racism of Whites therefore fundamentally kept them from understanding was that intellectual ability and intelligence were not the same things and were not even necessarily correlated, that reason or reasoning logic were not the same as rational thinking or rationality. Reasoning logic could be employed with irrational beliefs and thinking to try to verify them and to try to carry these beliefs and thinking to their logical conclusions, as religious beliefs and religious thinking so easily demonstrate.*

But Whites were not daunted by the great inadequacy of their thinking. They believed, owing to their racist beliefs and thinking, that they were superior to Blacks, especially in cerebral capability. But as strong as this belief was, and it was very strong in the nineteenth century in America among a wide range of people and among intellectuals in Europe, it did not close down the issue for Whites. Because Whites always felt they had to prove these contentions. But why? If Whites felt they were inherently and cerebrally superior to Blacks, why would they have to prove it? Why would they not just accept their beliefs and let it go at that? Why, for instance, would southern white slaveholders pass laws making it illegal to teach Black slaves to read and write when they believed that the slaves lacked the intellectual ability to learn to do these things? What was the motivation for this kind of behavior? Or the motivation generally among Whites to keep proving what they already considered to be true and a permanent, unchangeable condition between themselves and Blacks? Because it was permanent and unchangeable, this condition transcended time and history. In any period in American history, the situation would be the same.

But the reality of the situation was different. And it was this reality that Whites had to confront and deal with from time to time, but they could only usually deal with in a racist manner, inasmuch as that was what most were. They had to deal with the fact that there were individual white intellectuals who did not accept the idea that Whites were inherently cerebrally superior to Blacks and who said so publicly. And then there were the Black people themselves whose intellectual capability they witnessed or heard about. Thomas Jefferson believed that Black people were inherently an inferior people, not just intellectually, but also emotionally, but his racist thinking was sharply rebuked by Benjamin Banneker, a Black scientist from the state of Maryland, in a critical letter. In the nineteenth century, Whites were startled to discover that there were some ex-slaves who had the intellectual ability to write books or nonslave Blacks who published and wrote for newspapers or were very articulate in public speaking—articulate in attacking racism and slavery. And then there was the most threatening and alarming confrontation of all: knowing of or hearing about a Black person or persons who had graduated from a college or university. This threw a huge wrench in the racist fantasy mill.

But white racists also had a way of bouncing back from these threats to their racist beliefs and what they also knew was a threat to their rationales and justifications for why they were on top in America and why they dominated Blacks and why they had numerous opportunities to develop and advance in America and Blacks did not. They invariably and quickly turned to the *exception explanation*. There were individual Blacks who were exceptions. But most Blacks did not fall into this category. They clearly were inherently inferior. But how were the exceptions to be accounted for? For Whites, it was simple. The exceptional Black person had a white father. That accounted for their intelligence. Suppose the person had a Black father, but the latter was not around to be seen. The answer would still be that a white father was involved because the Black person demonstrated intellectual capability. But suppose both parents were Black, and their offspring was decidedly Black and demonstrated intellectual capability? White racists would just ignore that question and would either ignore or avoid a Black person or Black persons like that.

But in the nineteenth century, white people in America really had a problem, particularly in the late part of the century. Blacks, alone or with White help, established public schools and laid the foundations for colleges and universities. Blacks had White public or private schools and White colleges and universities to emulate. They did not have to start from scratch in regard to the problem of administration in public schools, colleges, or universities or the kind of teachers needed at all the different institutions or the kind of curricula to have in them. Blacks were establishing the means, more so than at any other time in their history in America, to educate themselves, to nourish and develop their intellectual abilities and intelligence, and even to produce elites among themselves. And then there were some northern Blacks at the time who were graduating from some of the prestigious colleges and universities in that region, that is, from Harvard, Yale, and other top institutions. And there were many more Black writers of articles and books, many more Black newspapers and editors and journalists. The intellectual superiority of Whites was being seriously challenged, and it would be challenged even more in the future, when the Black colleges and universities became that in fact, not just in name. The Black public schools, as well as Black colleges and universities, would stand as *anti-racist* structures in America; they would also be forms of Black Power, specifically forms of institutional Black Power, that could augment their structural and power capacities. A perception could be made of a close association among Black Power, Black intellectual capability, and Black intelligence, associations that numerous Whites could see, and which, functioning as racists toward Blacks, they had to thwart, suppress, or eradicate.

The latter was not now possible. But thwarting and suppressing Black educational institutions, or Black anti-racist structures was possible. Whites in the late nineteenth century went at these tasks most viciously. They publicly promoted white supremacist, but especially ebonicistic racist beliefs, in a manner they had never done before, with great denigration of Black people and their public images and specifically a great denigration of their intellectual capability, likening it to animal intelligence and using and perverting Darwin's theories to argue the point that Blacks were arrested in their cerebral and general anatomical development, which kept them permanently at the subhuman or animal level. The southern state legislatures and county governments, drawing in this and similar racist thought, made certain Black public schools and colleges and universities got very little public money. Blacks had to rely upon their nickels and dimes and the generosity of northern white philanthropists and middle-class white donors, whom Booker T. Washington induced to be generous.

And Whites turned to science to help them to discredit Blacks and particularly their intellectual capability. So desperate were they to do this that they turned to what they regarded or convinced themselves was a science, craniology or skull size measuring, or in present-day parlance, craniometry. Harvard biologist and geologist Stephen Gould wrote in 1974, "The racist arguments of the nineteenth century were primarily based on craniometry, the measurement of human skulls. Today, these contentions stand totally discredited. What craniometry was to the nineteenth century, intelligence testing has been to the twentieth."[2]

The turn to craniometry had been desperate, because it had been an effort to try to salvage something from the "science" of phrenology that had been discredited in the 1840s. The phrenologists had measured and studied skulls. They had also divided the human brain "into separate faculties, each of which dealt with a specific emotion, sentiment, or power of reasoning. In general the size of a particular part of the brain indicated the extent of power, and the size of the individual faculties could be ascertained by an examination of the head or skull."[3]

The phrenologists had argued that the different races of the world had different head shapes. But they also argued that different head shapes appeared in the same race. The head shape indicated the cerebral organization and, thus, the size and functional capacity of the brain. The larger the brain, the greater its organization, complexity, and intellectual or mental functioning. The Anglo-Saxons, the phrenologists had argued, had a perfectly shaped head and, therefore, the largest and most complex brain and also therefore the greatest intellectual capability. Germanic peoples, or Teutonics, were next in line. The Irish were further down the line in brain size, organization, and intellectual ability. But all white people had better-shaped heads, larger brains, and greater intellectual ability than people of color, especially black people and Black people. Phrenology had been a reflection of White intellectual capability at work, and it had produced a worthless pseudoscience, of extreme unintelligence. And by the 1840s, there had been Whites who had declared phrenology a pseudoscience, an expression of unintelligence.

But in the late nineteenth century and even into the twentieth, there were white physicians and white physical scientists, individuals with intellectual ability, who turned to craniometry, or skull measuring, arguing this time that a larger skull indicated a larger brain and, therefore, greater intellectual ability. A problem with this craniometrical explanation was that many animals had larger skulls than human beings, which logically should have invested them with a greater brain size and greater intellectual capability. But this was clearly absurd. It finally became clear that this new craniometrical science and its explanations were absurd. What racist white physicians or scientists were never able to perceive as absurd was how cerebrally inferior white women gave birth to cerebrally superior white men. It would seem, logically, that such men would have to be at least half cerebrally inferior, which would further mean, logically, that neither white men nor white women nor the white race itself was capable of significant intellectual ability or intelligence. These would have been devastating thoughts, totally destructive of White racist thinking and feelings of natural superiority. This kind of thinking could not be indulged in and had to be avoided at all costs. And it was, consciously and unconsciously.

The unintellectual character of craniometry brought forth some new white male intellectuals who took up the subject of race, innate endowments, intellectual ability, and intelligence. Most of these men were social scientists. The latter were emerging in America with the growth of social science instruction in colleges and universities, and they saw themselves as intellectuals, as specialized kinds of intellectuals, such as sociologists, psychologists, or anthropologists, who felt they had a moral and social obligation to provide the American public with scientifically gathered social knowledge. These white social scientists were usually racists, and thus much of the social knowledge they brought forth was vitiated. Those white social scientists, usually white men, who took up the subject of race and the questions of innate qualities, particularly innate intelligence—as it was usually described—were not free of racism, as could be discerned in their written accounts. But these white male intellectuals went to a different argument. Indeed, they returned to what they regarded as the scientific argument of the eighteenth-century Enlightenment, that environment had a great deal to do with human intelligence. They were not as sanguine about the effects of environment on intelligence, not as absolutist as Enlightenment thinkers, but environment played a very large role in the matter. These thinkers also implicated genetic endowment in the development and display of intelligence. Du Bois joined with these white social scientists in expressing these views and put the two thoughts together, along with others, to construct his scientific sociology.

But he developed his sociology against a strong White racist back-drop, one that had white people maintaining two fundamentally different kinds of social-cultural environments in America, one for white people and one for Black people. The one for white people provided all the possible opportunities for intellectual, social, and cultural development. The one for Black people, which white people, thinking and acting as racists, consciously and determinedly severely curtailed in each of these areas. This was traditional racist behavior: creating an environment for Whites to grow, develop, and prosper in and an environment for Blacks to be stunted in, which made individual and group progress and development difficult and as slow as possible, and where deprivations and suffering always outstripped opportunities and prosperity. The two different environments were *racist structures*, one to benefit Whites, one to exploit Blacks for White benefit and to severely reduce Black benefit in America. The idea was to make sure that the Black environment did not function to augment the intellectual ability or intelligence of Blacks, which, of course, would be related to the social and cultural development of Blacks and their competitive capabilities in America. Whites well knew the role their own environment played in augmenting their intellectual capability and their competitiveness in society. But their racism said to them that they could not mention environment for themselves and certainly could not focus on it as a large factor. This would be saying to Blacks that environment was very important to intellectual, social, and cultural efforts and outcomes. Whites, compelled by their racism, had to cover up or downplay the environment as a determinant element and emphasize inherent or innate characteristics of Whites and Blacks, indicating, of course, publicly, loudly, and often, that White innate attributes, especially White innate cerebral capabilities, were superior to Black innate attributes, especially Black innate cerebral abilities. But as in the past, racist beliefs were not enough to convince fully or fully to stand by. This was at best belief and faith, which produced racist assumptions. Proof had to be had. Science was the only way to provide the proof. But all the sciences and scientific explanations had been discredited, had been declared pseudoscientific and unintelligent. Social science research was somewhat helpful, but it was also dangerous. It focused on the environment in a large way. Staying away from the environment and the notion of environmental determinants was crucial. But where to turn? Miraculously, a place was found. A race (racism) savior was found: intelligence testing.

It was not immediately a godsend. Such tests were initially administered individually and so did not disclose much about groups or group intellectual differences. Then the testing was done on groups and produced a scare for white racists. Group testing was administered in the army, on American soldiers. After the First World War, the results of the testing were published: "the Army's point scores were translated into mental age levels. . . . According to the scales and the method of calculation then in use, it turned out that the average Army draftee had a mental age of fourteen years."[4] But an even more devastating, or at least an equally devastating blow to white racists was that some northern Black soldiers scored as high as some northern white soldiers, and higher than most southern white soldiers. The tests had been drawn up in relation to formal school education. This meant that some northern Black soldiers had had schooling equal to a number of northern white soldiers, and better schooling than most southern white soldiers (and, of course, most southern Black soldiers as well). This clearly meant that environment played a large role in determining intelligence. That was something that the testers could not readily accept—that they did not want to accept, and they were racked with confusion. Whites, generally, lived in a better environment than Blacks, but white soldiers registered a mental age of fourteen on the intelligence tests. It was believed that something was wrong with the construction of the tests.

Today various kinds of intelligence tests are in use, and they have been refined and refined. The two most popular are the Stanford-Binet and the Wechsler intelligence tests. Both tests have been developed for children and adults and over many years have been administered to both. The Wechsler tests have a standard deviation of 15 percentage points, which gets translated into an intelligence quotient, or IQ, number, which theoretically or presumably indicates the level of intelligence. Average intelligence on the Wechsler test is 100. Since the standard deviation is fifteen percentage points above or below the average, 115 would be the above-average figure and 85 would be the below-average figure. The Stanford-Binet test also has 100 as an average for intelligence but has a sixteen-point standard deviation, making 116 an above-average score of intelligence and 84 a below-average score of intelligence. What this kind of testing today reveals is that most Blacks consistently score below the average intelligence, specifically, fifteen points below the average. The Stanford-Binet and Wechsler tests were initially administered and refined on white people in the United States. Thus the figure of 100 as the average intelligence score was equated with the average intelligence of white people, and white people themselves were above and below the average intelligence.

But the total White orientation of the two main IQ tests said a whole lot that the testers did not want to hear. What they mainly did not want to hear was that these tests were developed and administered in a racist, that is, white supremacist/ebonicistic–inundated society that reflected a White domination of Black people, conceived to be a permanent situation in America, a domination rationalized on the basis that white people were inherently cerebrally superior to black people and Black people. This was both a racist belief and a racist assumption. And the power of this belief and assumption on the users of the two intelligence tests was that they initially tested them on white people, not even thinking to test them on Black people. This means that these tests were environmentally based, that is, on the White cultural and social environment in America. The tests reflected and were geared to that environment, that is, to the kind of thinking that white people did, the kind of logic they employed to think and analyze, the kinds of beliefs and values they had, and the kind of cultural and social objectives they had or were encouraged or compelled to pursue. This meant, with no room left for questioning, that intelligence tests, in terms of their construction and content focus, and the object of giving the tests and the results hoped for or expected from them, had a very strong environmental base, orientation, and motivation. It could not be otherwise.

And if it were believed and assumed that Black people were less intelligent than white people, then it would be believed and assumed that they would score significantly below Whites on intelligence tests. There might be some Blacks that would score high, but most would score rather low. On intelligence tests developed by white people for white people, Blacks who scored highly or more highly than most Blacks would most often be those Blacks who were born, raised, and educated in an environment that was similar to that of many upper-range Whites taking the tests. Most Blacks would not be from that kind of environment and naturally would not do as well as some other Blacks and most Whites who had taken the tests. And every time white people and White environment–oriented intelligence tests were given to Blacks, most Blacks would score less than a number of Blacks and most Whites on those tests. If there were a fifteen-point difference one time, there would be a fifteen-point difference, or some other constant lower figure the next time and the next time and the next time, until something changed. This would necessitate more Blacks moving out of the environment characterized by low scoring and into an environment where other Blacks lived characterized by high or higher scoring or that the environment of most Blacks was radically transformed and sustained in its radical transformation and commensurate to the environment of higher-scoring Blacks or the environment of Whites.

One thing is clear: there is no such thing as a universal intelligence test. There has never been a universal cultural and social environment on this planet. The planet reflects a mosaic of cultural-social environments. Intelligence tests produced in different cultural and social environments would be the bane of people taking these tests from other environments. It is possible for a country or countries to take on some of the culture and social life of another country or countries, by borrowing aspects of their culture and social life and making them part of their own existence. This would invest the borrowing countries and peoples with some of the same thinking practices and reasoning logic and some of the same beliefs, values, and cultural and social goals as the borrowed countries. There could even be a fanaticism on the part of borrowing countries to make borrowed traits part of their countries and the lives of their peoples, because of feelings of their need or indispensability: for military purposes, for economic, scientific, technological, or administrative purposes. Intelligence tests from the borrowed countries, taken in the borrowing countries, would likely show similar test results. Test scores might even be higher in the countries that borrowed cultural and social traits and invested them in an intensive or fanatical manner in their culture and social life and in their peoples.

The Stanford-Binet and Wechsler tests came under heavy criticism from Blacks, and also from some Whites. But the most devastating criticism of the tests came from white people who research and study intelligence and administer intelligence tests, who saw the serious limitations of these testing devices. The tests, as these individuals indicated, had essentially the same content and were administered in the same traditional manner, ignoring new learning theories, new testing items, and downplaying the role of environment in forming and developing human intelligence.

One major limitation of intelligence tests is their failure to grow conceptually with the advent of important advances in psychology and neurology. The items in the Stanford-Binet . . . are essentially the tasks that were developed by Binet and his collaborators Henry and Simon in France near the turn of the century. Wechsler's Verbal subtests are close analogs to tasks conceived in Binet's laboratory; some of his Performance subtests also resemble Binet items, and all of them have their roots in the nonverbal test batteries in use about a half century ago. This historical perspective is not intended to demean the genius of Binet or the innovative contributions of David Wechsler. But the fact remains that the impressive findings in the areas of cognitive development, learning theory, and neurology during the past 25–50 years have not invaded the domain of the individual test. Stimulus materials have been improved and modernized; new test items and pictures have been constructed with a keen awareness of the needs and feelings of both minority group members and women; and advances in psychometric theory have been rigorously applied to various aspects of test construction, norming, and validation. However the item content and the structure of the intelligence tests have remained basically unchanged.[5]

Fifteen years after these comments, reflecting on the refinements of the standard intelligence tests, psychologist Ken Richardson wrote that not much progress had been made in understanding or measuring intelligence:

Strange as it may seem, this is precisely the situation with the phenotype we call intelligence. As we have seen throughout this book, there is little agreement about what the intelligence phenotype is. Indeed, not only do presuppositions vary about how best to describe it; even within the IQ tradition almost anything "mental" seems to pass muster as a measure if it predicts scores with approximately the "right" kind of correlations with other criteria. Even the more recent information-processing theorists, adopting a more traditional scientific logic, seem content to accept a bewildering variety of measures as descriptors of the phenotype. These include things like digit span, vocabulary, analogical reasoning, verbal comprehension, deductive reasoning, general knowledge, and so on. The fact that we have no clear purchase (let alone one that permits measurement) on the phenotype, is also testified by the fact that contemporary views of the "real" intelligence phenotype range from mental speed, through error-free transmission of nerve signals, to "power" of metacomponents, and so on.[6]

And as to genes and their relationship to intelligence, Richardson remarked that "we don't know anything about the genes underlying intelligence; either how many there are, of what sort, whether they vary from person to person, and if so to what extent, with what consequences and importance for development, and so on."[7] And the change in this outlook did not show immediate promise.

The above sets of comments by researchers on and writers of intelligence show the serious problems and inadequacies of intelligence testing even after extensive refinement, including the most serious problem and inadequacy: *there is no scientific basis on which to conduct such tests.* There is no consensus among people professionally and scholarly interested in the subject on what constitutes intelligence. So what is measured by all the testing? How can something be measured accurately, let alone scientifically, that cannot be clearly defined and has a multiplicity of definitions? Intelligence testing makes no distinction between what I have called in this chapter *intellectual ability* and *intelligence*, which are not the same thing and may not even be correlated. There is no way to determine scientifically whether genetic inheritance or environment plays the larger role in either intellectual ability or intelligence or, scientifically, which factor plays the largest role in individual or group results. There is no scientific way and thus no scientific evidence to indicate clearly and decisively the intellectual potential of a single gene or a cluster of genes. There is no way scientifically and thus no scientific evidence to indicate how many genes in the human brain are related to intelligence. There is no scientific proof, and no scientific proof can be gathered, to determine how many genes are required for one point of intelligence or even what is a point of intelligence. To say that the genetic inheritance, the g factor in human intelligence, swings forty points, between a minimum estimated low of forty and a maximum estimated high of eighty points, as Arthur Jensen said years ago and many testers still rigorously cling to, is hardly a scientific observation or explanation. If the g factor was at 40, then that would mean that the environment factor, the e factor, would be 60 percent of intelligence. If the g factor was 80, then the e factor would be 20. But why can't the measuring devices establish something that doesn't swing or swing so much, for example, that the g factor is 60 percent or 75 percent or that the e factor is 60 percent or 75 percent? And, in any case, how can the g factor be 40 points, or 80 points of intelligence when it can't be determined scientifically how many genes equal a point of intelligence or what a point of intelligence is? Another question to be asked is what is the scientific proof that the g factor relates to intelligence and not to intellectual ability, and vice versa. On the face of it, someone should be cautious in talking about the scientific evidence for the presence of the g factor in intelligence when the range for error is 40 points, not 3 or 4 or 5. This sounds like speculation and guesswork more than anything. And, to stay with my critical assessment, it cannot be established scientifically what structure or quality of cultural and social environment is requisite for augmenting intellectual ability or intelligence. It cannot be established scientifically that a given environment is equal to x number of genes, so that it can be determined scientifically that the genetic and environmental factors are equal or disparate contributors to intellectual ability or intelligence. Measuring intellectual ability or intelligence cannot be done scientifically. What intelligence tests can produce is scores on tests, even predict scores on tests. But what the test results will not and cannot indicate, as a scientific measurement, is the clear and decisive extent of g or e in the results; nor can they show the clear and decisive way that they combined to produce results. Nor will the tests clearly distinguish which played the larger role in tests results, intellectual ability or intelligence, or what was the combination of the two elements that produced the results on tests. Intellience tests are a pseudoscience and can't be anything else, because they will always be without a scientific foundation from which to be constructed and tested.

But white people want intelligence tests, so we have them. There is that fundamental, primordial racist need to prove to themselves that they are innately superior to Blacks, physically and cerebrally. This relates to their need to justify to themselves why they are on top in America and Blacks are on the bottom (so they will not have to look at other reasons as to why this is so) and to that other racist primordial need of being able to say to themselves that they are guiltless, innocent, and nonresponsible for the depressed situation of most Blacks in America. White racists have used pseudosciences before over their history in America to provide rationales and justifications and to assuage and satisfy deeply and critically felt racist needs. As subtle racists, still with racist cognitive patterns, considerable racist psychological traits and afflictions and continuing strong racist needs, they will continue to search for and employ pseudosciences. Instead of giving children and youth intelligence tests, they should be evaluating or assessing children's knowledge of various subjects, their critical intellectual skills, to see how well they do and where their knowledge and skills are. This would indicate something about their intellectual abilities and intelligence. What the results of diagnostic assessments would also indicate to teachers is what they have to teach students to help them understand and master skills and subjects. This would be a way for intellectual ability and intelligence to come together. It would be a way, from childhood to youth, from preschool to high school, to bring intellectual ability and environment together to help produce intelligence. Specifically it would be a way at every school level to determine where the best teachers should be utilized, with renumeration reflective of the large and challenging assignment. Intelligence testing works strongly against a motivation to teach and the good teaching of large masses of America's children and youth. Those who do not score highly on the tests end up in remedial classes, classes with little intellectual stimulation or encouragement or significant intellectual activity, to say nothing of instruction or educational materials that promote the encouragement and development of intellectual ability and intelligence. Children and youth who score highly on intelligence tests are put in an instructional process that has a middling to low educational content and stresses acquiring certain knowledge, certain intellectual perceptions, and certain analytical skills, that will prepare them to take exams, such as the Scholastic Achievement Test, to which the instructional process is geared. A formally educated child or youth or a formally educated adult is not synonymous with great brain power. There are people with manifest brain power and not much formal education. And their lack of formal education, cultivation, or sophistication shows.

But the lack of understanding and miseducation goes on, and the pushing of White interests and White needs goes on to the exclusion or suppression of other people's interests and needs, especially those of Black people. But it also excludes and suppresses the needs of America. Intelligence testing has never functioned much in the interests and needs of America. It has always functioned—and continues to function—mainly in the interest and needs of White racist America.

9.

Racism and the Question of Intelligence II

A recent book that has been widely read and continues to spark controversy told the American public, implicitly rather than explicitly, that intelligence testing will continue to serve the interests and needs of White racist America. This was said implicitly by a psychologist (recently deceased), Richard Herrnstein, and a sociologist, Charles Murray, in their large and provocative book *The Bell Curve*. These authors indicated their strong favoring of intelligence testing and made it clear that they favored the traditional tests and rejected the criticisms of the traditional Stanford-Binet and Wechsler tests for children and adults and also the tests conducted by Arthur Jensen. Indeed, the authors stayed away from or played down testing results that contradicted or threw serious doubts on their contentions. They even decided that there was only one way to look at intelligence. They arrived at this view not by an examination of intelligence or even by trying to synthesize the myriad views into a single view. They took an idea from Harvard psychologist Howard Gardner and other scholars, who had said that problem solving was central to intelligence, which they converted into being the only way to look at it:

> For Gardner, as for many other thinkers of intelligence, the notion of problem solving is central. "A human intellectual

competence must entail a set of skills of problem solving," he writes, "enabling the individual *to resolve genuine problems or difficulties* that he or she encounters and, when appropriate, to create an effective product—and also must entail the potential for *finding or creating problems*—thereby laying the groundwork for the acquisition of new knowledge."[1]

This view of intelligence is not central and is very limited. It is not even a view of intelligence. It is a view of intellectual ability, but a limited view of intellectual ability. Critical analysis is a form of intellectual ability, and a necessary one. People are not always solving problems; they are not even usually doing so. Most often people are engaged in thinking, individual behavior, social interaction with others, participation in institutions and cultural activities, engaging in play, or working at jobs or occupations that are rather routine and repetitive. But they must be able to evaluate the things that they say, that they think, that they hear, in which they participate, the social relationships they have, the social situations they step into, the television programs they watch, the reports from teachers about their children. These are all mundane things, of course, but they are the things of human existence, that make up human existence on a daily basis. And the purpose here is to avoid problems, not to make or cause them—and certainly not to go looking for any. Critical evaluation for understanding, critical evaluation for facilitating, critical evaluation for better participation, or for greater enjoyment, or critical evaluation for greater input, for example, into discussions, family activities, or community activities is where the human mind is mainly intellectually engaged.

Herrnstein and Murray, like other people they knew about, were not interested in the kind of intellectual ability I just described, which I regard as very central to human functioning. Like any intellectual ability, it has to be guided by intelligence, which also helps to develop intellectual ability. Knowledge is critical to intelligence, but so are imagination, sensitivity, openness, morality, and even emotional control or stability—a number of ethical and affective qualities that philosophers and even many psychologists like to rule out for intelligence, so that their understanding of intelligence is intellectual ability. But it also has to be said that intellectual ability is also augmented especially by affective human qualities or lessened by their meager inclusion or application.

But clearly when the focus is on problem solving, then the interest in applying intellectual ability and the intelligence that can be developed to aid it, and vice versa, is in restricted areas, namely, in science and technology and places or situations where these things are applied, such as in scientific and technological research, production or economic strategies, marketing, organization construction or functioning, or administrative activities. This kind of intellectual activity focuses on things, procedures, processes, or problems or on the use of equipment, facilities, or other kinds of resources. People are not the focus of this kind of intellectual ability or the intelligence associated with it, which guides it or helps to develop it. When the focus, for some reason, turns to people, it induces people to be seen as *problems* and who are to be dealt with as if they were *problems*. This is pure devaluation of human beings and humanity—pure dehumanized thinking. It shows how science and technology are closely related to racist thinking and racism. But it is more than just a closeness. Western science and technology, that is, the advancement in these things in the seventeenth and eighteenth centuries, which laid the foundation for the Western World's superadvancement in science and technology, occurred at the same time that Whites/Europeans were engaged in exterminating and subduing Indians and conquering the Western Hemisphere; they were engaged also in a horrendous African slave trade, using African slave labor and the slave labor of descendants of Africans in the Western Hemisphere. The wealth derived from this horrendous and continuous exploitation was used to help finance the development of science and technology. These instruments of power were then used against Indians and Africans, rationalized by racist beliefs and assumptions that Indians and Africans were not human beings, but nonhumans or subhumans, or Non-Others. They were considered to be things or problems to be dealt with, and with the scientific and technological capacities that went into weapon making and warfare, into ship construction and navigational devices, that went into communication devices, that went into agricultural production using slave labor, or which went into the marketing of slave-produced agricultural products or business techniques to facilitate this marketing and trade. Racism, science, and technology were wedded together in Western civilization in the seventeenth, eighteenth, and nineteenth centuries, each stimulating the conception, development, and use of the other, individually or in tandem. America was a prime exhibitor of these kinds of realities.

In America (as well as in Western Europe), white men are the prime exhibitors of the kind of intellectual ability or, as Herrnstein and Murray would say, of the kind of intelligence associated with problem solving. They dominate and control America's science, technology and the technological research going into them, corporate economic institutions, the bureaucracies of governments, economic corporations, and other powerful institutions; they mainly design the rules, procedures, or processes involved in the use of science and technology and in the functioning of institutions. They are also the Americans who mainly think of people in this country as *problems*. White men have shown much skill over the history of America in problem-solving capabilities, exceeding that of other Americans, mainly because they have monopolized the conceptions, the rules or procedures, the scientific and technological practices, and the institutions where this kind of intellectual activity predominated in America. But in social matters, white men historically have shown less intellectual ability and less intelligence; trying to build and sustain a society where one part would be slave and the other nonslave is a prime example, as are their efforts to build a rational society on an irrational foundation and to build a just and moral society on a foundation of immorality and injustice. The problem-solving ability of white men was innate, that is, genetic; but it was also environmental, indeed, an acute environmental situation, because it was an essentially monopolized situation. As to which played the larger role, the g factor or the e factor, it cannot be said with any certainty; and it is not particularly important to know, unless it is assumed or accepted that only white men have the intellectual capacity for problem-solving intellectual activity. White women, many Black men and women, and many Asian men and women have demonstrated the falsity of that notion, even on traditional intelligence tests.

A reason that Herrnstein and Murray stressed that intelligence was centered in problem solving, other than the fact that they had a limited conception of intelligence, was that it also enabled them to talk about what they called in their book the *cognitive elites*, which to them was a new social element that had emerged in America with the kind of intelligence that they said was intelligence. They did not call this new elite an intellectual elite, or an elite of intelligence. They argued that they did not even like the word *intelligence*, saying it carried too much political baggage. They preferred the term *cognitive ability*, that is, the cognitive ability to do problem solving. Their preferred term for intelligence led to the term *cognitive elites*.

The cognitive elites, the authors said, were those bright young Americans whom traditional intelligence tests identified; they graduated from America's most prestigious colleges and universities, moved into America's most prestigious and best-paying occupations, and joined with traditional rich and powerful people in America to help lead the country. These cognitive elites were mainly white and mainly white men. There were some Blacks among them as well, about 100,000, out of a population of over 30 million people. These Blacks scored high on the traditional intelligence tests, at 125 points, well beyond the 100 point average. "One hundred thousand is a lot of people. It should be no surprise to see (as one does everyday) blacks functioning at high levels in every intellectually challenging field."[2] When it is considered that the authors talked of 7 million cognitive elites in America, with Whites making up the overwhelming part of that number, it is not clear what this seeming praise of Black cognitive elites was about, especially since the authors did not see Blacks adding substantially to that number, because they concluded that most Blacks scored well below 125 on the traditional intelligence tests, even well below the mean score of 100. Moreover, they argued that an environmental change or improvement would not help this situation or these Blacks much. Indeed, the primary reason that they did not think that even a positive environmental change would help most Blacks was because, in their view, most Blacks were genetically inferior. How did they prove that? Their proof, as they presented it, was that the g factor was the most important determinant of intelligence (based on that unscientific view of genetic intelligence fluxuating forty points, between forty and eighty points of intelligence), and because Blacks consistently scored 15 points less than Whites on traditional intelligence tests (drawn up by white people, mainly for white people), and the notion that an ability in problem solving equalled intelligence, which indicated that Blacks had less innate intelligence than Whites.

The authors actually had a problem in regard to the matter of environment, or the e factor in intelligence. They had to give it some recognition, though they clearly did not want to. There were Blacks in a middle-class environment indeed, from the same kind of environment that many Whites were from who scored high on intelligence tests, who scored high on intelligence tests repeated twice. This indicated that environment and the *e* factor were strong determinants of intelligence, even their limited conception of intelligence. The authors were back at that situation of the intelligence tests administered to white and Black soldiers during World War I, where many northern Black soldiers scored higher than southern white and Black soldiers and as high as many northern white soldiers, indicating the strong role of environment in intelligence. The earlier testers did not like the test results turned in by a number of northern Blacks and were determined not to see those kinds of results again. Herrnstein and Murray had a problem with the scores of Black middle-class people that pointed to a strong *e* factor. What they did was to say arbitrarily and pontifically that an improved environment would not help most Blacks improve their intelligence; the authors played down environment to be able to emphasize the *g* factor in intelligence, which they said was low in most Blacks. They also downplayed the environment of Whites to be able to emphasize the *g* factor among them, which they said was high.

But the environment that Herrnstein and Murray really played down in regard to Whites was the historical environmental factor, or what I call the *h e* factor. That historical environment went back to the seventeenth century. It was an environment that said that white people were godly or godlike; that said that they were the only Americans and that America was theirs; and that gave them most of the opportunities in America for education, jobs, occupations, and high incomes, as well as opportunities for good housing, good neighborhoods, good public services, and good health and medical care, and the most opportunities for power, prestige, and social position in America. That environment has kept evolving in America up to the present day. This was the environment in which most Whites now lived and the one in which intelligence tests were administered to them.

There was another historical environment in America as well. This was the Black historical environment, which was characterized by an earlier form of slavery that lasted for 230 years. This environment also saw laws passed saying that Black slaves were not to be taught to read and write. There was strong daily racism that denigrated the intelligence, the character, and the physical and spiritual being of Black people and daily assaulted the psychology and psychological strength of Black people. There were also racist laws and segregation for Blacks, slave and nonslave. And then, in the late nineteenth and early twentieth centuries, millions of Blacks were returned to another form of slavery through legal, economic, and political means such as losing the right to vote, and by physical violence and terrorism. There were also the exclusion and segregation that Blacks had to endure, South and North, and always a low wage or a low salary, usually less than Whites got for doing the same kind of work. There was the determined effort to make certain that Blacks did not gain much public money for public school or higher education, and there was an equally determined effort to keep Blacks from becoming important financial or economic elements in America. This broad environmental condition underwent change, sometimes through accidental situations, as when Whites fell out with each other and Blacks could take advantage of the situation to make political, economic, or educational gains or when Blacks engaged in actions in their own community to change matters or in political actions against Whites to open up opportunities for themselves and to improve their cultural and social existence in America. The changes in the Black community, from the nineteenth to the twentieth century, up to the present day, produced a Black middle class and a Black middle-class environment. The Black middle-class environment was one of education, culture, wealth, social opportunities, and a higher standard of living; the Black lower-class environment was one of low education, poor diet and nutrition, high unemployment, great poverty, high crime, poor housing, neighborhoods, and social services. From these backgrounds Blacks were drawn to be given intelligence tests—tests made for white people and the kind of environment they lived in, which nurtured them.

Herrnstein and Murray paid absolutely no attention to the historical environment of Whites or Blacks in America or to these two separate h e factors in their discussions about intelligence tests, White and Black intelligence tests, or about the g factor related to Whites and Blacks. Why were these two critical factors omitted? It certainly was disengenuous to do so, given how the authors stressed the g factor and indicated how it strongly differed between Whites and Blacks. The authors projected the view that they were being objective in their discussions, that they were not racists, not seeking to project racist sentiments. But this flagrant denial of environmental realities for Whites and Blacks raises some serious questions about scholarship and its intent. There can be no doubt that saying that Blacks were genetically inferior to Whites in intelligence fell right in line with the historical White racist view and obesession about Blacks being inferior in this way. And using intelligence tests, a "scientific" device, to prove it, falls in line with the other attempts that white racists had made to use science to validate the inherent inferiority of Blacks. But the authors endeavored to move away from charges of racism and racist intentions with their book by saying that they expected a convergence of intelligence test scores between many more Blacks and Whites, although expected this to take place about the middle of the twenty-first century. And it would mainly be between Blacks from the Black middle class and Whites of a similar class status.

But for the authors to show even this amount of optimism for the future meant that they had to be making the assumption that White racism was not presently very strong in America and that it would be almost an insignificant factor or even totally over by the middle of the twenty-first century. One is forced to say that if the first assertion is right, then the only conclusion possible is that denial had been working strongly in the authors. And if the second assertion is right, then it has to be said that the authors had been very naive, if not downright fanciful and delusory in their thinking. But there was another reason for Herrnstein and Murray's optimism. It sprang from their lack of a significant understanding of American history and American social life, that is, American society. They evidenced in their book that they knew very little about racism, about Whites as racists, and about White racism's impact on American history, culture, and social life. This is not a criticism just to be laid at their feet. It could be laid at the feet of many white scholars, including white sociologists. There are also Black and other scholars of color who show similar limitations. For instance, Herrnstein and Murray wrote in their book, "Social class remains the vehicle of social life, but intelligence now pulls the train."[3] Some Black intellectuals or Black scholars, thinking of themselves as Marxists or radicals, would subscribe to this view. They simply are not understanding the historical sociology of America or the sociology of American society, past or present. Social class has never been the primary vehicle of status, opportunities, wealth, or power in America. Since the seventeenth century, white men have dominated white women in this country. This was not class domination, but rather gender domination. Gender status and gender power were the vehicles of social life. These vehicles continued on in American history, but others were added, namely, racial status and racist privilege. Another vehicle was added that embraced all of these elements. This was the White over Black hierarchical racist social structure and social system (which had originally exhibited racial hierarchy), which will be spoken of subsequently as the White over Black structure and system, or simply as the structure and system. This structure and system were established in the late eighteenth and early nineteenth centuries in the British colonies. This was the general social structure and social system of the colonies. The White over Black structure and system passed into the new United States and became the general social structure and social system there. It was through this structure and system that individual, group, and social action took place in America. Thus, this structure and system functioned as the fundamental means to reproduce American history, culture, and social life.

First, the White over Black hierarchical structure. It had a top and lower part, with Whites on the top and Blacks on the bottom. The top part was constructed by Whites usurping American culture, American social classes, and American social institutions and calling them *white* or *white American culture*, white or white *American social classes*, and *white* or *white American social institutions*. They also called the top of the structure, as a collective expression, *white society* or *white American society*. White people invested American culture, American social classes, and American social institutions with a strong dose of white supremacy/ebonicism, making them function in a strong racist manner. At the bottom part of the reproductive structure were Black people and their culture, their social classes, and their social institutions. Collectively, the Black community or "Black society" comprised the bottom of the hierarchical structure. The two parts of the American hierarchical structure interacted with each other when Whites, as individuals, as part of groups, in social classes, or through institutions interacted with Blacks or when Blacks as individuals, from social classes, from institutions, or as a group interacted with Whites. This interaction took place primarily in the White-usurped American culture and social institutions but also at the bottom of the hierarchical structure, as when Whites entered Black social-cultural life. The interaction between Whites and Blacks and the top and lower parts of the White over Black structure produced the White over Black social system. This structure and system still function in a fundamental way in America, now inundated mainly with subtle White racism, and remain the fundamental way that American history, culture, and social life are produced, sustained, and perpetuated.

What the hierarchical structure and system have clearly and deter-minedly produced and reproduced over time is the white male dom-ination, control, and exploitation of America. White men have done this as racists, particularly white supremacists/ebonicists, but also by expressing other forms of racism and by treating other people in America, including white people, in a racist manner. They have expressed their racism individually and from their gender group, through American culture, American social classes, American social institutions and, collectively, American civilization. As said in the last chapter, Black conservatives never talk about white men and their power and domination in America. White female feminists are com-pelled to talk about these realities, but they usually do not do so directly; usually do not say *white* males or *white* men. They usually use words or phrases such as *men* or *males* or *power elites* or *ruling elites*, or such phrases as *good old boys, good old boys network*, or the words *patriarchy* or *capitalists*. The indirect language reflects the fact that white feminists do not like to think or talk about racism. They seldom anymore use the words *sexist, sexists,* or *sexism,* denoting male racism, and, thus, white male racism toward white women (and other women in America). So many white female feminists are afraid of exposing their own racism, particularly their white supremacy/ebon-icism. The racism of white female feminists, which is a general reality among them, makes them vulnerable to white men who can manip-ulate it to their advantage.

While the White over Black structure and system is the general, fundamental way that white men reproduce their power and domi-nant position in American history, culture, and social life—this *racist-inundated structure* and *racist-inundated system*—they also do this with specific manifestations of the structure and system. Two things in particular: the *white male racist affirmative action practice* and *white male racist quotas.* Throughout American history, white men have seen to it that white men have had the encouragement, the political and legal backing, the financial backing, the opportunities, the education, the connections, the placement, and the experience to aspire, to achieve, to attain status, power, and wealth, and to domi-nate, control, and lead America. This historical white male racist af-firmative action effort always produced a large quota of white men ready to take advantage of the support and opportunities made avail-able to them, which resulted in large quotas of white men attaining wealth, status, power, and positions of domination and leadership in

America. White men still practice white male racist affirmative action in a vigorous manner and still produce large white male quotas in the areas stated above. This all has to be done now, for the most part, by the subtle use of racism and racist power and by specific subtle racist manipulations of culture. One such subtle racist manipulation of culture is intelligence testing.

Intelligence tests, in Europe or America, have been devised and administered mainly by white men. The research that has gone on to produce these tests and refine them has been done mainly by white men, who have also mainly interpreted the results of such tests. In America (as in Europe), intelligence tests are a reflection of white men, a reflection of the image and worth they have of themselves. The tests reflect the white male understanding of thinking, of logical methods, of the proper ideals, beliefs, values, what constitutes intelligence, knowledge, and social understanding, what individual character and individual aspirations and goals should be, and what constitutes individual and public morality in the country. Intelligence tests, especially the traditional standard tests, are consciously and unconsciously designed to reproduce the mind, character, and social perceptions of white men in white men and in all other people in America as well (in short, *cultural cloning*). White men dominate and control America's culture, social classes, and major national or societal institutions, and through these structures, blatantly racist at one time and now mainly subtly racist, they are the ones who primarily offer work, remuneration, positions, power, and domination or leadership roles to a very large number, if not most, of other Americans. To those Americans most like themselves, in mind, character, skills, and social understanding, they proffer America's largesse; this means to white men, first, and then to other Americans as they see fit, unless forced to alter their order of preference. This has always been the meaning of the historical phrase *a white man's country*. And no way could this ever be interpreted as other than a racist phrase. Which also means that intelligence tests devised primarily by white men, and administered primarily by white men (or white women, who think like white men), are white male racist based and oriented. The emphasis on problem solving is not neutral. This is the white male method of thinking in America. It's the kind of thinking that is not just problem oriented, but thing oriented, that socially thinks of people as problems, as property, as numbers, as things, invariably as something other than human beings. Black people have a history of being victimized by this kind of thinking, a history of centuries of being regarded as chattel property, as nameless and faceless entries in plantation or small slave farm ledgers, as, collectively, the "Negro problem" or a "social problem." It is the kind of thinking that functions today in the American economy, that focuses on Blacks and other people—including white people—not as people, but as dollar signs, profits, or profit margins, or as bottom-line entries, tax deductions, tax write-offs, production costs, cost cuts, or downsizing or right-sizing items. It is the kind of thinking that is found in social science research and study, that is peopleless oriented, that substitutes things such as hypotheses, theories, statistical groupings, statistical categories, statistical results and statistical predictions, for people. Physical science seeks to dominate or, at least, to control physical nature and to make use of it under methods of control. Social science seeks information that would make it possible to dominate and control people and their thoughts and social behavior, which is what it fully means to be able successfully and with great accuracy—to predict the thought and social behavior of people. Human beings are very complicated, ruled by thoughts, dreams, aspirations, impulses, emotions, and so on. To be able to successfully predict what people will say or do means that large chunks of humanity have been stripped away from them, leaving them much like inanimate objects. Any social science that seeks to predict, that is, to control human thinking and social behavior, and not just to disclose valid information about individuals and groups or social situations is ill-conceived. It does not, to put it strongly, understand how this kind of social science thinking, research, and writing is predicated on racist thought, thought that is compelled to strip people of their humanity to think about them or to relate to them. It has to be remembered that contemporary Western physical and social science grew up with White racisms, which had profound effects on them. Phrenology and craniology reflect this truth. White men in America have historically shown a lack of or a very low level of *social intelligence*. The latter, like any form of intelligence, is hard to define. Knowledge and experience suggest that it includes intellectual ability, but also knowledge, various kinds of relevant ideals, beliefs, and values, various kinds of sentiments, much imagination, much sensitivity, much humaneness, a strong conscience, and a strong morality. It would be no more possible to measure social intelligence in a scientific way than individual intelligence can be measured in this way. But both can be established as ideals and as individual and social motivations and guidances, that is, as universal ideals or principles or motivations for Americans and America. The ancient black African theologian St. Augustine had established a long time ago that when people knew the truth, or what was virtuous, it did not mean that they would act on these understandings. They might well act, and rather often, in just the opposite ways. So, so much for trying to predict human behavior, as a main social science enterprise. There was also the fact that people could change their behavior after learning certain facts or about certain projected consequences. What *is* a worthy objective for social science is endeavoring to disclose as much knowledge, truth, and understanding as possible about human beings that would make individual and group behavior more intelligent and social programs more intelligent and helpful. This kind of orientation and these kinds of objectives characterized W.E.B. Du Bois's scientific sociology.

All of what I have said above relates to America's historical, cultural, and social future, and especially as the authors of *The Bell Curve* envision it, in which America will be "color-blind"—having gotten back to that orientation—and in which cognitive elites would play a large dominant or leadership role, along with traditional rich and powerful and dominant elements in America. As a point of order, almost, it has to be said to the authors of *The Bell Curve*, and to the readers who sucked on the point, America has never been a "color-blind" society. It began as a color-oriented society the day white people looked upon the color of Indians as a *problem* for themselves. In the 1860s and 1870s, when Black chattel slavery was ended, and when Blacks, according to amendments and laws, attained citizenship and political civil rights, it was said that America was a "color-blind" society. And all the while this was said, white supremacy/ebonicism remained alive and kept renewing and strengthening itself until it was fully dominant again. In the 1960s and 1970s Whites, like white people in the 1860s and 1870s, and similarly, right after the passage of statutory laws, said America was a "color-blind" society. But subtle White racism confirmed the naiveté, as well as the self and group delusory thinking, and the personal and group lying of that view. It also revealed the will, if not indeed the compulsion, of most Whites to keep promoting racism in America. As the dean of Black historians, John Hope Franklin, wrote in *The Color Line* in the early 1990s: "A color-blind society eludes us. For one reason, we have not sought diligently and continuously to pursue it. . . . For another reason . . .

we as a nation do not . . . appreciate what constitutes a color-blind society. . . . A final reason . . . is that we do not wish to find it.[4]

The primary argument of *The Bell Curve* was that there was a new social element on the American scene, functioning as a dominant and leading social element, one which would grow more numerous in the future, and perhaps, even more powerful in the future. This new group of elites was not necessarily a blessing for America. It was made up of bright people, but they also had a strong streak of social insensitivity and social indifference about them. Herrnstein and Murray had simply been wrong in saying that cognitive elites were a new social agent in America. They were thrown off by their own narrow notion of cognitive elites, whom they saw as a social element associated only with advanced technology. "A true cognitive elite requires a technological society."[5] Cognition has never been associated just with technology. It can be traced back, in its most elemental forms, in the early and millennial hominids. It can also be located in early, as well as many present-day animals. Throughout the millennia of human history and human life, and specifically, and certainly, throughout America's centuries-old history, it has been associated with all manifestations of culture and social life. Cognition, after all, involves thinking, logical methods, imagination, perception, intuition, and I would say even vision and feeling and psychological, as well as neurological means to acquire knowledge and understanding. Cognition is an attribute of all human beings, not just intellectuals or individuals with great cerebral power. A given individual could have several cognitive systems, which some psychologists call schemata, functioning in his or her general psyche or general psychology, cooperating with one another or functioning separately from one another to deal with specific and limited reality. Thus, unquestionably, every human society is a cognitive society. It cannot be otherwise.

Many contemporary societies have intellectuals who are engaged in cognition in a more intense and analytical manner than most other people in such societies. They create various kinds of intellectuals, with various kinds of roles for them to play, to carry out their intense and specialized cognitive activities. The following kinds of intellectuals can be found in many contemporary societies, playing cognitive social roles and carrying out cognitive activities: scientists, technicians, scholars, philosophers, literary critics, fiction writers, poets, playwrights, artists, teachers, journalists, and so on. These are the cognitive elites of many contemporary societies, to distinguish them from the mass of people of such societies, who also engage in cognition, but less intensively and less profoundly as a rule.

America, in its early centuries, had the kind of cognitive elites referred to above. Most of them were white men. And these white men, these cognitive elites, joined forces with white men of power, wealth, and high social position to dominate and lead in what was initially the British colonies. Indeed, some of the rich and powerful were also cognitive elites in the British colonies, such as John Jay and Thomas Jefferson. There were also individuals in the colonies who were not rich, but who were powerful and among the dominant leaders, who were cognitive elites, such as Benjamin Franklin and Alexander Hamilton. What this understanding makes it possible to say is that "a true cognitive elite" is not new in American history and society; a cognitive elite joining with rich and/or powerful elements to lead jointly is also not new. These social realities emerged and functioned in the British colonies, and the realities and functioning passed into American history and social life. And in both of the historical-social contexts, the fused leadership elements consciously engaged in white male racist affirmative action, and the denigration, suppression, and restriction of others, namely, white women and Black men and women, who had to be made even to see the futility of trying to gain access to America's largesse.

Richard Herrnstein and Charles Murray, like other white male and female conservatives, and also like Black conservatives, were against affirmative action. The two authors referred to this as an artificial and unfair method of advancing Blacks or other "minorities." Joined by Black conservatives, they seemed totally oblivious to the historical and continuing white male racist affirmative action and white male racist quotas, as well as how these practices had greatly helped to produce the large number of white male cognitive elites in the country. The two authors blithely commented that if affirmative action, or that which they argued and understood to be affirmative action, which came into existence in the 1960s, were removed from higher education, there would be a much smaller number of Blacks and other minorities attending the most prestigious colleges and universities in America, making the latter in the future, even more than they are now, White institutions instead of American institutions. This did not seem to bother the authors at all, who said, nonchalantly but sincerely, that Blacks and other minorities could find their place and road to advancement studying at the second level of prestigious colleges and universities in America. This kind of casual and indifferent attitude also fell across the mass of Americans, whom they described as the vast American "underclass," and who the authors said would be able to find their secure and dignified place in the country as the permanent bottom of American society. Herrnstein and Murray expressed concern that the cognitive elites were callous and indifferent toward the mass of people in America and would also be in the future. But one gained the impression that this was not something that particularly distressed them.

White men, especially in America, attack what is commonly understood as affirmative action and quotas while other white men, behind all kinds of erected barriers, carry out these twin historical and interlocking racist practices, which effectively produce *white male entitlements.* The continuation of these practices and entitlements (abetted by Blacks and others who usually do not refer to them, raise questions about them, or do not assail them) continues to show that white men do not like to compete against Blacks, white women, and other people of color—but particularly against Black men and Black women. Over the history of America, various forms of oppression—such as slave laws and slavery, racist laws and racist segregation, intimidation, violence, and the use of elements of culture in an oppressive manner, such as science, technology and, throughout this century, intelligence tests—were used to eliminate and/or reduce competition between white men and Black men and women. Herrnstein and Murray could not see, and certainly did not advocate, that laws, social policies, and social programs that ended white male racist affirmative action, white male racist quotas, and white male racist entitlements, and therefore, the white male domination, control, and exploitation of America—and opened up more opportunities, more power, and more wealth to other Americans—would be something that America would greatly appreciate, that would make it feel one with itself, and not estranged from itself. But it would take Americans identifying with America, and not White racist America, to make this come to past.

10.

Cognitive Elites and American Division

The authors of *The Bell Curve* expressed their concern about a serious division occurring in America. They saw this division as one between the cognitive elites and what they called the vast and growing underclass in America. To these authors, this represented a serious class division. Since they saw it as a permanent thing or at least something of very long duration, it might better be described as a structural division. But in reality, there is no such structural division in America, because there is no underclass in America as these men described it and also because there is no cognitive elite social class as Herrnstein and Murray described that. The cognitive elites are individuals who can be found in gender groups, ethnic groups, social classes, institutions, or social organizations. They also form, collectively (in a loose manner), a social group. Karl Marx had a way of describing social or economic groups as social classes. This had been a long-standing practice in the Western world; but Marx and his intellectual followers, whether they were communists, socialists, or liberal thinkers influenced by Marx's thought, made it very commonplace. Gunnar Myrdal, a Swedish social scientist, strongly influenced by Marxist thinking, perhaps invented the concept *underclass* in a book of the early 1960s: *Challenge of Affluence*.[1] At the time Myrdal employed

his term, Sweden had a hierarchy of social classes, as did other countries in Europe, as did the United States and Canada. It was indeed
a social reality around the world. In a hierarchical organization of
social classes, all classes below the first one are "underclasses." Thus,
such classes are not a post–Second World War phenomena in Europe,
or America, or Canada, although they are considerably the product
of the science and advanced technology of Western countries, or of
science, technology, or organizational structuring and functioning of
big corporate economic institutions. What Myrdal and others after
him, influenced by him, depicted as an underclass to be found in
many Western countries, however, was not created by science, technology, and economic transformations; such an underclass does not
exist in Europe and America—or elsewhere in the world. In Canada,
America, and Western European countries, in particular, but also in
some other countries with advanced industrial and commercial economies, large numbers of people in the lower class increasingly lack
the education, technical, or economic skills, even some of the pre-
requisite psychological traits required to function in the contemporary
economy. There is a future danger that most of the lower class, or
the entire lower class of some countries, will be permanently dysfunctional this way. That class will also bulge over the years, because
similarly dysfunctional people in the middle class will fall into its
ranks, as is presently happening in America, Western Europe, and
elsewhere.

The American situation, though, has its own distinctive characteristics beyond what I have described as the increasing and dangerous
reality plaguing other countries. This was not something that Herrnstein and Murray were able to fathom. They, like others before them,
had generally misunderstood the phenomenon of the underclass.
They also had a different view of the origins of the underclass than
had Myrdal and others. The latter had seen the origins stemming
from the scientific, technical, and organizational transformations in
Western economies. Herrnstein and Murray saw persistent low scoring on intelligence tests as the source of origins for America's underclass. So, according to these two authors, intelligence testing had
created social classes in America, classes totally disparate from each
other, with different kinds of futures ahead of them. One had a future
of opportunities, wealth, power, and privileged position; the other
had a future of extreme and permanent subordination, over-
crowdedness, poverty, and public denigration and disdain. But these

authors were and remained in favor of intelligence tests and their playing such an overwhelming role in deciding the future of people in America. They said the American people had to learn to live with inequality, even permanent inequality. America has never stood for inequality as an ideal, though White racist America has always stood for inequality as an ideal—a permanent, transcendent ideal. Social thought in America that advocates inequality as an ideal comes out of America's racist history and reflects racism, no matter how subtly it comes across. Writing about the efforts of racists to deny equality in America in the 1970s, John Hope Franklin remarked:

> One supposes that the whites who were resisting the efforts of blacks to enjoy equality were actually operating from the premise that equality could not be shared. Since they assumed that blacks occupied an inferior position in the social order, they believed that equality could not and, indeed, should not be divided between blacks and whites. To the extent that they believed equality could not be divided they were perhaps correct. To the extent that they believed equality could be arrogated to one segment of society and withheld from another segment, they were woefully mistaken. Equality could be shared, but it could not be divided in a way that some would be more equal than others.[2]

Herrnstein and Murray were willing to divide equality in a very extensive manner, not only between Blacks and Whites, but among Whites. In the history of the American South, white slaveholders, then new white slaveholders and industrialists and merchants in the late nineteenth and early twentieth centuries, created and maintained a large number of Whites in the region as unequal "poor Whites." Now Herrnstein and Murray were content to see the existence of a large number of "poor Whites," by the scores of millions in America, thinking that this would be acceptable to them and America. It would be, as it has been historically, acceptable to White racist America. If people in America have fought against use of the vote to prevent their equality in America, why would the authors of *The Bell Curve* think that they would willingly accept and not fight against test scores? This is not a very intelligent assumption or observation.

But as reflected in their conception of cognitive elites and the mass underclass, Herrnstein and Murray failed to show an understanding of the construction of American society. The latter was a creation of intelligence tests, an abstract, artificial creation, not an extant social reality. The cognitive elites were not a social class, but were, as said, individuals to be found in gender groups, ethnic groups, social classes and other social formations; collectively, they were a social group, but not necessarily one that would act in concert. For instance, cognitive elites among Blacks, among Poles, among Japanese, or those who are found in the upper class or middle class would not necessarily seek to form a general alliance with one another. Indeed, there would be barriers against doing that.

What Herrnstein and Murray never saw was the White over Black hierarchical structure and system that still existed and functioned in America, and rather effectively. This structure and system had, in the twentieth century, expanded into a broader White over People of Color hierarchical structure and system, with the White over Black portion still the centerpiece of them and still the primary reproductive part of them. Because of the broad White over People of Color structure and system, America has white underclasses and people of color underclasses. This reflects the strong racism that still exists in the country and the complexity of American life.

The primary social division in America, however, is still between Whites and Blacks, as has always been the case in American history and social life and as is the division that is moving into the future. The white sociologist Andrew Hacker had a perception of the main division of America, between Whites and Blacks, and this division carrying on into the future. In *Two Nations: Black and White, Separate, Hostile, Unequal*, he wrote:

> Black Americans are Americans, yet they still subsist as aliens in the only land they know. Other groups may remain outside the mainstream—some religious sects, for example—but they do so voluntarily. In contrast, blacks must endure a segregation that is far from freely chosen. So America may be seen as two separate nations. Of course, there are places where the races mingle. Yet in most significant respects, the separation is pervasive and penetrating. As a social and human division, it surpasses all others—even gender—in intensity and subordination.[3]

Hacker published his book in 1992. Herrnstein and Murray published theirs two years later. One author saw what two other authors could not see. One author observed American society and came up with a view of it. The other two authors looked at intelligence test scores and then proceeded to construct a society for America that existed in their heads and book, but not on the American continent. But Hacker was only partially right in what he saw taking place in America. There was a division between Whites and Blacks, all right, that White racist segregation had helped to produce. But it was not a division between "two nations." The question of one American nation, indivisible, had been settled in the mid-nineteenth century, and the settling of the matter had been bloody and final. This does not mean that America is a country that is structurally strong and together, because it isn't. Recently white historian Arthur Schlesinger, Jr., blamed Blacks and other people of color in America's colleges and universities for threatening division of the country by their insistence on some silly and dangerous notion of "multiculturalism" in American higher education and in American social life. Multiculturalism was a direct attack against White racism, especially the racism against people of color. Schlesinger could not see that. He wrote in his book *The Disuniting of America*: "*E pluribis unum*. The United States had a brilliant solution for the inherent fragility of a multiethnic society: the creation of a brand-new national identity, carried forward by individuals who, in forsaking old loyalties and joining to make new lives, melted away ethnic differences."[4]

The Latin phrase *E pluribis unum*, strictly speaking, was a reference to the states that came together in the latter eighteenth century to form the United States and was not a reference to ethnic groups. But of course it could be stretched to embrace ethnic groups. The "brilliant solution" that Schlesinger referred to was not a brilliant solution at all. It was an ordinary solution. Nation-states in Europe and other places in the world had been put together and had been held together, with the aid of a single national identity, loyalty to which did not require forsaking all ethnic loyalties, just those that interfered with implementing and sustaining the national identity and constructing and sustaining the nation-state. The fact and reality that those ethnic groups which came to the United States did not forsake all their "old loyalties" is reflected in the continuing existence of ethnic groups in the country and the existence of a multiethnic American society. Schlesinger was chanting the "American exceptionalism"

song with his comments, with his book and with his fears that the
country would be destroyed by multicultural politics and social action. The real "exceptionalism" that Schlesinger did not see about
the United States, which other historians and other scholars have not
seen either, is the White over Black structure and system that was not
found in European countries and functioned in America as the "brilliant solution for the inherent fragility of a multiethnic society." What
the advocates of multiculturalism were doing, and still seek fundamentally to do, other than to attack White racisms, is to get White
people to admit and accept the fact that people other than white
Europeans have contributed to the cultural and social history and life
of America. These are things that Schlesinger and other white Americans have great difficulty acknowledging and accepting. But it also
has to be said that a number of multicultural or multiethnic advocates
approach identity or difference matters in an either-or or more-than
manner, meaning that they try to eliminate the country's *American*
identity or the country's cultural and social *Americanness* or endeavor
to subordinate them to multiculturalism or multiethnicity. These
kinds of specific identities and realities are possible precisely because
of what America is and stands for. White racists are to be condemned
for trying to eliminate or suppress or weaken America and its universal
ideals, and multicultural and multiethnic advocates and politics are
also to be condemned when they endeavor to so the same. America
has to have universality or, at a minimum, consensus for itself, which
does not preclude pluralism or diversity and which is all attainable
with the proper cognitive method, which doesn't slice things up in
an either-or or more-than manner.

Back to Andrew Hacker. The critical division he had not seen,
which involved racism and racist segregation, and which had strongly
helped to produce it, was a deep—and dangerous—structural division. The latter is characterized by Black people and other people of
color overwhelmingly living in big and small cities and white people
increasingly overwhelmingly living in suburbs and small towns. This
division is marked and symbolized by the Expressway of the American
highway system, which separates two sociophysical segments of America. The last time a structural division was this pronounced and dangerous in America was when northern Whites were divided from
southern Whites by what historian Lerone Bennett, Jr., called the
Cotton Curtain. Now it is the concrete Expressway. And the division
is not between groups of white people, but between white people

and Blacks and other people of color. Some will no doubt regard this as pessimism or alarmism. But when attention was drawn to it by the *Kerner Commission Report* in 1968, thirty years ago, and virtually nothing has been done to interdict or end the division, then it seems quite necessary to bang the alarm bell. It is also necessary to do this when one observes how so many Whites deny that racism still exists strongly in America and how so many Whites are still prone to "substituting a pleasant falsehood for an ugly disagreeable truth, and of clinging to a fascinating delusion while rejecting a palpable reality." Or, as Du Bois had said, for "getting rid of a problem [rather] than . . . solving it." And the bell clearly has to be rung when one contemplates what Richard Herrnstein and Charles Murray said about young white male cognitive elites acquiring and playing national, regional, and local leadership roles in the country. This element will function overwhelmingly from the sociophysical (or geographical) base of suburbs and small towns. By that fact and reality alone, they will help to solidify and perpetuate the present racist-racial structural division in the country. They will be nourished and reinforced in their racism, which strongly characterizes suburbs and small towns, by what white politicians, political analysts, and journalists like to refer to as Middle America, which is a euphemistic and cover-up phrase for Middle White Racist America. The white male and female cognitive elites living in a subtly racist environment will pass this subtle racism onto their children, who will pass it onto their children. The racist-racial structural division will harden like concrete, if it does not cause a racial and thus national breakdown before that. Individual and social intelligence would say we must not let that happen. They would also advocate taking major steps to end the great division. But this is the worrisome side of the danger. White male cognitive elites have and would have a limited understanding of intelligence and even less understanding of social intelligence. White presidential, senatorial, and gubernatorial candidates have been getting elected over the last decades by manipulating the racist-racial structural division in America. Their candidacies have been conducted with strong subtle racist orientations, in that transparent guise of "conservative" (or even middle-of-the-road) politics and by batteries of coded racist phrases and subtle racist images, making millions of Whites feel that they are *better* and *different, more useful to America* than *those* people and happy that they and their children are separated from them. Political candidates and sitting politicians fan these frightful, callous, and indifferent attitudes and feelings and abet and also harden the racist-racial structural division in the country by proposing on television, on the stump, or in government bodies to cut away money and social programs from people of color in the cities, projecting the proposals and cuts in racist coded language, such as "curbing spending," "welfare reform," "family values," or "liberal policies" and getting their subtle racist constituencies to buy their language and proposals and to support their candidacies or efforts in governments.

Monies or social programs withdrawn or pared down will only aggravate already depressing socioeconomic conditions of cities and the depressed lives of so many people, and this will reinforce negative racist conceptions about people in the cities. Few Whites will see any connection between withdrawn or pared-down monies and programs and greater social and cultural deprivations among Blacks and others in cities. They will explain the laws, policies, and programs in ways that satisfy themselves, that establish in their minds the legitimacy of their actions, and that will make them feel that traditional White racist feeling of being guiltless, innocent, and nonresponsible for the increased deprivations. And the great deprivations themselves, and the socially debilitating behavior that will flow from them in the cities— the consequences of racist thoughts and actions—will then, again in typical White racist fashion, be used to rationalize and justify the thoughts and actions. Indeed, there are Whites now, usually academics, and usually sociologists, who back away from writing and talking of the "inherent inferiority" of Black people or other people of color to avoid being called racists. They have shifted the racist or "inherent inferiority" argument from people to the environment in which the people live. Poor socioeconomic environments are naturally "inherently inferior." Who can deny it? So the environment can be blamed, not people. The espousers of this view can even project an image of themselves as reasonable or sensitive or progressive in their thinking, as well as an image that they wish to be helpful to those that the environment has ravaged and continues to ravage. They might even talk publicly about altering or improving a ravaging environment. But the subtle racism of this kind of thinking and imaging becomes discernible when these espousers of humaneness and justice *oppose* programs or efforts to change debilitating environments. All in favor of the objective but unable to accept any means to pursue it. This is the kind of thinking and social behavior that Black people have had to endure for centuries in America. It has always been difficult for them to interact with a people who have demonstrated such little capacity to relate to them intelligently, responsibly, humanely, decently, and with a sense of conscience, morality, justice. There is no reason to be optimistic about a changed or improved situation when contemplating the white male and white female cognitive elites who will exercise power and leadership in America. Their education at the first- and second-line prestigious colleges and universities in America will give them virtually no understanding of racism, what it is and how it functions. There certainly will be no understanding of how racism has affected Whites and how Whites, injecting and maintaining various kinds of racism in American history, culture, and social life, have effectively poisoned and vitiated these tributaries. Whites complain loudly and often about the lack of values, standards, and public morality but are incapable of seeing the primary role that they themselves have played in this degenerative situation. The everyday language of America today in conversation, social interaction, and institutions is mindlessly vulgar, profane, and even pornographic and is on the verge of being used extensively in college and university classrooms by instructors and students, with the horrendous destruction this portends for higher education. The responsibility for these situations can be placed precisely at the feet of white people—traceable to the time when masses of white people, cutting across gender, ethnic group, class lines, and even age, *learned how to swear and be profane and vulgar in public*. And that moment can be traced back to the movie *Who's Afraid of Virginia Woolf?*, with its absolute disregard for the Third Commandment, and the many subsequent movies, theatrical productions, and comedy forums that became the vehicles of public instruction in profanity, vulgarity, pornography, and disrespect for ideals, beliefs, and values. This is all passed off as "adult language," "adult content," and "adult behavior" in movies, dramas, and other media. The plunge into degeneracy in America is called realism or being honest or truthful. Whites had always perverted American ideals, beliefs, values, and morality. Now they are in the process, indeed leading the process, of utterly destroying American public morality and public discourse, for which they wish to accept no responsibility. Indeed, the kind of people that Americans and America should be able to rely on to protect, nourish, and preserve written and spoken American English, such as playwrights, actors, writers, poets, professors, teachers, and others, are the very ones engaged in vitiating and subverting the national language. These are other things that white male and female cognitive elites will not learn in the prestigious colleges and universities. They certainly will learn nothing about the racist-racial structural division in America, what has caused it, what sustains it, and its great danger for the country. And certainly nothing about how to end it. They will learn just the opposite along these lines. They will learn how to deny the existence of the structural division, while at the same time unconsciously or indirectly learning how to maintain it and to harden its lines even more. What they will not learn in school, they will learn living in the subtle racist environments of the suburbs and small towns and the way these two relate to the cities and the people in them; or they will learn when they participate as politicians, legal counsel, consultants, or bureaucrats in state governments or state agencies that regulate and serve cities.

A fact that subtle white racists as well as other white people will have difficulty accepting, is that America has never been put together very well. It has been characterized by poor social construction. The White over Black hierarchical structure and system is the most obvious proof. Another proof was constructing a country between the late eighteenth and first half of the nineteenth centuries on the basis of one part being slave and the other part being nonslave. A horrendous war resulted from this poor construction. And then in the late nineteenth and early twentieth centuries, as if nothing had been learned at all, Whites made an effort to return to the situation prior to the war by returning millions of Blacks to another form of slavery in the South and then massively suppressing the political and civil rights of the Blacks who were not slaves in the region while at the same time trying to promote a "free" northern region of the country, as had been done prior to the mid-nineteenth-century war. The poor social construction continues today, with a racial-physical structural division. All of these manifestations of poor social construction have been manifestations of White intellectual ability and White intelligence. This is what the white cognitive elites have inherited, an inheritance passed onto them through their schooling at every level; it will be preserved and passed on in the subtle racist suburban and small-town environments in which they live.

It is clear that the future of America cannot be left solely in the hands of white people, not even predominantly in their hands. In their hands, it is not America that will be primarily constructed and perpetuated, but primarily White racist America. In the hands of the white cognitive elites, America will be White racist America. This clearly means that Blacks cannot be passive or indifferent to the future direction and development of America. America's future is their future, and if they are not active in vigilance, thought, and action, there will be an effort to make America's future without them, an effort to continue denying and subordinating most Blacks in America as it moves along in time. Blacks, acting as individuals, will not be able to stop this denial or subordination. Individual Blacks will be able to advance culturally and socially in America's future. The White over Black structure and system will accommodate that, as it has done throughout its existence in America. But that structure and system have always functioned in a strongly suppressive manner to make certain that most Blacks did not use America's culture and social institutions in a direct manner for benefit as some Blacks and most Whites were able to do. Recently, black sociologist Orlando Patterson stated in his book, *The Ordeal of Integration*, that two-thirds, or most Blacks in America had achieved a middle-class status.[5] This is not only wrong, the scholar provided statistics proving that his contention was wrong. He remarked: "If we use a medium income of $36,000 as the cut-off point for middle class, then 36 percent of Afro-American families may be considered middle class."[6] That means that 64 percent, or nearly two-thirds of Black families, are not middle class, with most falling below the medium figure. He continues: "My own calculations . . . show that at least 35 percent of Afro-American adult male workers are solidly middle class. The percentage is roughly the same for adult female workers."[7] Hence, 65 percent of adult male and female workers are not middle class. Orlando Patterson, while correctly pointing to the changes that had occurred in America with respect to racism and the economic, social, and cultural advances of Blacks over the past 40 years, grossly exaggerated how much change had been made in both areas. Most Blacks still face strong White racism and are kept substantially out of America's largesse and away from the opportunities to dig into it. Like Black or black conservatives, the latter of which he is as a Jamaican American, he rejects or downplays group action to help Black or black people in America and regards individual effort as the panacea.

The mass of Black people are not going to make it in America on the basis of an individualistic social method. Nor can they rely on accidents taking place in history to help themselves advance, such as Whites falling out with each other and making opportunities available. They have to *rely* upon themselves, and other Black people, in short, the national Black ethnic community and the regional and local manifestations of that community. In short, and again, they have to *rely*, initially, primarily, and consistently, upon national Black ethnic community power and the regional and local manifestations of this organized and mobilized Black Power, and not some elitist "Talented Tenth" leadership as some say. Frederick Douglass once said in a speech: "No man can be truly free whose liberty is dependent upon the thought, feeling, and actions of others, and who has himself no means in his own hands for guarding . . . and maintaining that liberty."[8] He also said the following in a speech: "Power concedes nothing without a demand. It never did and it never will. Find out just what any people will quietly submit to and you have found out the exact measure of injustice and wrong which will be imposed upon them, and these will continue till they are resisted."[9]

As Douglass knew, it takes power to make the greatest and most effective demand on power and to extract concessions from it. That means it's going to take effective national, regional, and local Black ethnic community power to move against White racist power in America. This power is part of the White over Black structure and system and functions from it, specifically from the racist-inundated, highly centralized institutions that are part of that structure and system. These institutions will concede nothing, or only very little, without an effective Black Power demand. And that demand has to be made intelligently, imaginatively, with resolution, and with intelligent, imaginative ideological guides and political and programmatic action. The idea is to save, build, strengthen, and exalt America and not to maim, disgrace, or destroy it. This means that the progress, development, and freedom of Blacks in America, as a people, will require what has always been required: intellectual ability and intelligence and effective leaders and effective political action.

Blacks have to act collectively in America's future. They know better than most Whites what America is and what it stands for. They know better than most Whites when America is at its best. It is something that they can feel better than most Whites. That knowledge and that feeling are now required for America's future. Blacks have to be able to contribute significantly to the direction that America takes in the future and the content of that future. There has to be an effective Black participation to keep White racist America, the antithesis and negation of America, from monopolizing contributions to direction and content. The participation of Blacks has to be two-fold: organizing and using national Black Power within the national Black ethnic community to augment its aesthetic and social culture and its social institutions and social life and using the capacity of this community to aid individual Blacks in their development and advancement and the development and advancement of Black people as a people. The second kind of participation is to use organized national Black ethnic community power in an intelligent and effective way against White racist America, to endeavor to separate white people from it, so that white people, too, by the millions, along with Black millions, can make the effort to build the America that America, according to its own ideals and understanding of itself, wants built. Other people of color have to get in on this kind of participation and help to draw white people in. It will take years to construct this America. But even moving America forcefully and irrevocably in that direction—allowing no one or anything to reverse the process—will make it a better country for many, many people now left out of what America promises people and says they are entitled to as Americans. Blacks and others demonstrated that this kind of behavior can benefit many, many people when they pushed America toward its ideals and its genuine self in the 1950s and 1960s. Blacks have to keep America's hopes alive and keep on keepin' on. This has been a mission for Black people since the days when the Declaration of Independence, the Constitution, and the Bill of Rights declared America to stand for freedom, when Blacks decided that America was their home and that they were Americans, entitled as individuals and as a group of people to the benefits of this country, just as individual Whites and groups of Whites were entitled to the benefits. The Black mission continues in America. Its success or failure will represent the success or failure of the United States. Thus, it is crystal clear that for Blacks fully to succeed in America as a people, and for America to succeed in the future as the country it is supposed to be, it is going to take not only effective power on the part of Blacks (as well as others in America), but a rigorous, extensive, and continuous application of both individual and social intelligence. Indeed, individual and social intelligence have to be added to the pantheon of American ideals, beliefs, and values that define America and universal freedom in this country.

Notes

PREFACE

1. W.E.B. Du Bois, "The Souls of White Folk," in *W.E.B. Du Bois: A Reader*, ed. and with an introduction by Meyer Weinberg (New York: Harper & Row, 1970), 303.

CHAPTER 1: HISTORY: WHAT IT IS, WHAT IT TELLS US

1. Benjamin P. Bowser and Raymond G. Hunt, eds., *Impacts of Racism on White Americans* (Beverly Hills, CA: Sage Publications, 1981), 13.
2. Frederick Douglass, *The Life and Writings of Frederick Douglass, Volume 3: The Civil War, 1861–1865*, ed. Philip S. Foner (New York: International Publishers, 1952), 126.
3. W. E. Burghardt Du Bois, *The Suppression of the African Slave Trade to the United States of America, 1638–1870* (Baton Rouge: Louisiana State University Press, 1969), 198–99.

CHAPTER 2: RACISM MATTERS

1. Gordon W. Allport, *The Nature of Prejudice* (Garden City, NY: Doubleday, 1954).

2. W.E.B. Du Bois, "Prospect of a World without Racial Conflict," in *W.E.B. Du Bois Speaks: Speeches and Addresses, 1920–1963*, ed. Philip S. Foner (New York: Pathfinder Press, 1970), 124.

3. W.E.B. Du Bois, "The Negro and the Warsaw Ghetto," in *W.E.B. Du Bois Speaks: Speeches and Addresses, 1920–1963*, ed. Philip S. Foner (New York: Pathfinder Press, 1970), 253.

4. W.E.B. Du Bois, "Disfranchisement," in *W.E.B. Du Bois Speaks: Speeches and Addresses, 1890–1919*, ed. Philip S. Foner (New York: Pathfinder Press, 1970), 235.

5. W. E. Burghardt Du Bois, *The Negro* (New York: Oxford University Press, 1970), 90.

6. W. D. Wright, "The Faces of Racism," *Western Journal of Black Studies* 2, no. 4 (1987), 168–76.

7. Quoted in John Hope Franklin, *Racial Equality in America* (Chicago: University of Chicago Press, 1976), 50.

8. Quoted in John S. Haller, Jr., *Outcasts from Evolution: Scientific Attitudes of Racial Inferiority, 1859–1900* (Urbana: University of Illinois Press, 1971), 53.

9. Quoted in Jan Nederveen Pieterse, *White on Black: Images of Africa and Blacks in Western Popular Culture* (New Haven, CT: Yale University Press, 1992), 34.

10. Quoted in Martin Bernal, *Black Athena: The Afroasiatic Roots of Classical Civilization, Volume I: The Fabrication of Ancient Greece, 1785–1985* (New Brunswick, NJ: Rutgers University Press, 1987), 241.

11 Quoted in Anthony T. Browder, *Nile Valley Contributions to Civilization: Exploding the Myths, Volume 1* (Washington, DC: Institute of Karmic Guidance, 1992), 18.

12. Cornel West, *Race Matters* (Boston: Beacon Press, 1993).

CHAPTER 3: WHITE AND BLACK ALIENATION
IN AMERICA

1. W. E. Burghardt Du Bois, *The Souls of Black Folk: Essays and Sketches* (Greenwich, CT: Fawcett Publications, 1961), 16–17.

2. Ibid., 17.

3. Cornel West, *Prophetic Fragments* (Grand Rapids, MI: William B. Eerdmans Publishing Company, 1988), 48.

4. Quoted in Clinton M. Jean, *Behind the Eurocentric Veils: The Search for African Realities* (Amherst: University of Massachusetts Press, 1991), 13.

5. Bernard Lewis, *Cultures in Conflict: Christians, Muslims, and Jews in the Age of Discovery* (New York: Oxford University Press, 1995), 64–65.

6. Leonard P. Curry, *The Free Black in Urban America, 1800–1850: The Shadow of the Dream* (Chicago: University of Chicago Press, 1981).

7. As reported in Lee Sigelman and Susan Welch, *Black Americans' Views of Racial Inequality: The Dream Deferred* (New York: Cambridge University Press, 1991), xi.

8. "Poll Says Blacks Prefer to be Called 'Black' to African American," *Jet* 79, no. 17 (February, 1991): 8.

9. "Poll Reveals Black Prefer Term 'Black' to African American," *Jet* 86, no. 17 (August 1994): 46.

10. Frederick Douglass, *The Life and Writings of Frederick Douglass, Volume 2: Pre–Civil War Decade, 1850–1860*, ed. Philip S. Foner (New York: International Publishers Co., 1950), 192.

11. Alexander Thomas, M.D., and Samuel Sillen, Ph.D., *Racism and Psychiatry* (New York: Brunner/Mazel, 1972), 51.

CHAPTER 4: THE EXPERIMENT THAT NEVER WAS, 1783–1883

1. Nathan Irvin Huggins, *Black Odyssey: The African-American Ordeal in Slavery* (New York: Random House, 1990), lxxiii.

2. Robert C. Tucker, "Stalinism as Revolution from Above," in *Stalinism: Essays in Historical Interpretation*, ed. Robert C. Tucker (New York: W. W. Norton & Company, 1977), 79.

3. Despite the Seventeenth Amendment, senators still essentially represent states.

4. Winthrop D. Jordan and Leon F. Litwack, *The United States Conquering a Continent, Volume I*, 7th ed. (Englewood Cliffs, NJ: Prentice-Hall, 1991), 220.

5. Harry L. Watson, *Liberty and Power: The Politics of Jacksonian America* (New York: Noonday Press, 1990), 13.

6. Robert W. Johannsen, *Lincoln, the South and Slavery: The Political Dimension* (Baton Rouge: Louisiana State University Press, 1991), 91.

7. Richard Hofstadter, *The American Political Tradition and the Men Who Made It* (New York: Random House, 1974).

8. Eric Foner, "The New View of Reconstruction," *American Heritage* 34, no. 6 (October-November 1983): 15.

CHAPTER 5: THE ORIGINS AND LEGITIMACY OF BLACK POWER

1. Stokeley Carmichael and Charles V. Hamilton, *Black Power: Politics of Liberation in America* (New York: Random House, 1967).

2. Joel Kovel, *White Racism: A Psychohistory* (New York: Columbia University Press, 1984), 178.

3. Philip P. Hallie, *Cruelty*, rev. ed. (Middletown, CT: Wesleyan University Press, 1982), 104.

4. Adelbert H. Jenkins, *The Psychology of the Afro-American: A Humanist Approach* (New York: Pergamon Press, 1982), xv.

CHAPTER 6: YET TO LEARN ABOUT FREEDOM

1. Derrick Bell, *And We Are Not Saved: The Elusive Quest for Racial Justice* (New York: Basic Books, 1987).

2. Roy L. Brooks, *Rethinking the American Race Problem* (Berkeley and Los Angeles: University of California Press, 1990).

3. C. Vann Woodward, *The Strange Career of Jim Crow*, 3d rev. ed. (New York: Oxford University Press, 1974).

4. Peter Gay, *The Cultivation of Hatred: The Bourgeois Experience, Victoria to Freud* (New York: W. W. Norton & Company, 1993), 94.

5. Nathan Irvin Huggins, *Black Odyssey: The African-American Ordeal in Slavery* (New York: Random House, 1990), xvi.

6. Lerone Bennett, Jr., "Lincoln, a White Supremacist," in *The Leadership of Abraham Lincoln*, ed. Don E. Fehrenbacher (New York: John Wiley & Sons, 1970), 35.

7. Quoted in David Bartlett, *Life and Public Services of Honorable Abraham Lincoln* (Freeport, NY: Books for Libraries Press, 1969), 246.

8. Ibid., 197.

9. Ibid., 220.

10. Ibid., 219.

11. Cornel West, *Race Matters* (Boston: Beacon Press, 1993), 14.

12. Richard Majors and Janet Mancini Billson, *Cool Pose: The Dilemmas of Black Manhood in America* (New York: Maxwell Macmillan International, 1992), 1.

CHAPTER 7: SUBTLE WHITE RACISM

1. Michael Omi and Howard Winant, *Racial Formation in the United States from the 1960s to the 1980s* (New York: Routledge & Kegan Paul, 1986), 132.

2. William J. Wilson, *The Declining Significance of Race: Blacks and Changing American Institutions*, 2nd ed. (Chicago: University of Chicago Press, 1980).

3. Now at Harvard University.

4. Sharon M. Collins, "The Making of the Black Middle Class," *Social Problems* 30, no. 4 (April 1983): 369–80.

5. Bart Landry, *The New Black Middle Class* (Berkeley and Los Angeles: University of California Press, 1987).

6. Ellis Cose, *The Rage of a Privileged Class* (New York: HarperCollins Publishers, 1993).

7. William Julius Wilson, *The Truly Disadvantaged: The Inner City, the Underclass, and Public Policy* (Chicago: University of Chicago Press, 1987).

8. Barry Barnes, *The Elements of Social Theory* (Princeton, NJ: Princeton University Press, 1995), 32.

9. Shelby Steele, *The Content of Our Character* (New York: St. Martin's Press, 1990), 161.

10. K. Sue Jewell, *From Mammy to Miss America and Beyond: Cultural Images and the Shaping of U.S. Social Policy* (New York: Routledge, 1993), 27.

11. Robert Heilbroner, *Visions of the Future, The Distant Past, Yesterday, Today, and Tomorrow* (New York: Oxford University Press, 1995), 100.

12. Sidney M. Wilhelm, *Who Needs the Negro?* (Cambridge, MA: Schenkman Publishing Co., 1970).

13. John Walton, *Sociology and Critical Inquiry: The Work, Tradition, and Purpose*, 2nd ed. (Belmont, CA: Wadsworth Publishing Company, 1990), 265–66.

14. Patricia J. Williams, *The Rooster's Egg* (Cambridge, MA: Harvard University Press, 1995), 87.

CHAPTER 8: RACISM AND THE QUESTION OF INTELLIGENCE I

1. Reginald Horsman, *Race and Manifest Destiny: The Origins of American Racial Anglo-Saxonism* (Cambridge, MA: Harvard University Press, 1981), 46.

2. Quoted in Elaine Mensh and Harry Mensh, *The IQ Mythology: Class, Race, Gender, and Inequality* (Carbondale: Southern Illinois University Press, 1991), 13.

3. Horsman, *Race and Manifest Destiny*, 56–57.

4. Evelyn Sharp, *The IQ Cult* (New York: Coward, McCann & Geohaegan, 1972), 75.

5. Alan S. Kaufman, *Intelligent Testing with the WISC-R* (New York: John Wiley & Sons, 1979), 4.

6. Ken Richardson, *Understanding Intelligence* (Philadelphia: Open University Press, 1991), 117.

7. Ibid., 119.

CHAPTER 9: RACISM AND THE QUESTION OF INTELLIGENCE II

1. Richard J. Herrnstein and Charles Murray, *The Bell Curve: Intelligence and Class Structure in American Life* (New York: Free Press, 1994), 18.
2. Ibid., 278.
3. Ibid., 25.
4. John Hope Franklin, *The Color Line: Legacy for the Twenty-first Century* (Columbia: University of Missouri Press, 1993), 50.
5. Herrnstein and Murray, *Bell Curve*, 27.

CHAPTER 10: COGNITIVE ELITES AND AMERICAN DIVISION

1. Gunnar Myrdal, *Challenge of Affluence* (New York: Pantheon Books, 1963).
2. John Hope Franklin, *Racial Equality in America* (Chicago: University of Chicago Press, 1976), 95–96.
3. Andrew Hacker, *Two Nations: Black and White, Separate, Hostile, Unequal* (New York: Charles Scribner's Sons, 1992), 3.
4. Arthur M. Schlesinger, Jr., *The Disuniting of America: Reflections on a Multicultural Society* (New York: W. W. Norton & Company, 1992), 13.
5. Orlando Patterson, *The Ordeal of Integration Progress and Resentment in America's "Racial" Crisis* (Washington, D.C.: Civitas Counterpoint, 1997), 172.
6. Ibid., 22.
7. Ibid.
8. Quoted in Waldo E. Martin, Jr., *The Mind of Frederick Douglass* (Chapel Hill: University of North Carolina Press, 1984), 68.
9. Frederick Douglass, *The Life and Writings of Frederick Douglass, Volume 2: Pre–Civil War Decade*, ed. Philip S. Foner (New York: International Publishers Co., 1950), 437.

Selected Bibliography

Allport, Gordon W. *The Nature of Prejudice*. Garden City, NY: Doubleday, 1954.

Barnes, Barry. *The Elements of Social Theory*. Princeton, NJ: Princeton University Press, 1995.

Bell, Derrick. *And We Are Not Saved: The Elusive Quest for Racial Justice*. New York: Basic Books, 1987.

Bennett, Lerone, Jr. "Lincoln, a White Supremacist." In *The Leadership of Abraham Lincoln*, ed. Don E. Fehrenbacher. New York: John Wiley & Sons, 1970.

Bernal, Martin. *Black Athena: The Afroasiatic Roots of Classical Civilization, Volume I: The Fabrication of Ancient Greece, 1785–1985*. New Brunswick, NJ: Rutgers University Press, 1987.

Bowser, Benjamin P., and Raymond G. Hunt, *Impacts of Racism on White Americans*. Beverly Hills, CA: Sage Publications, 1981.

Brooks, Roy L. *Rethinking the American Race Problem*. Berkeley and Los Angeles: University of California Press, 1990.

Browder, Anthony T. *Nile Valley Contributions to Civilization: Exploding the Myths, Volume 1*. Washington D.C.: Institute of Karmic Guidance, 1992.

Carmichael, Stokeley, and Charles V. Hamilton. *Black Power: Politics of Liberation in America*. New York: Random House, 1967.

Collins, Sharon M. "The Making of the Black Middle Class," *Social Problems* 30, no. 4 (April 1983): 369–380.

Cose, Ellis. *The Rage of a Privileged Class.* New York: HarperCollins Publishers, 1993.

Curry, Leonard P. *The Free Black in Urban America, 1800–1850: The Shadow of the Dream.* Chicago: University of Chicago Press, 1981.

Douglass, Frederick. *The Life and Writings of Frederick Douglass, Volume 2: Pre–Civil War Decade, 1850–1860,* ed. Philip S. Foner. New York: International Publishers, 1950.

———. *The Life and Writings of Frederick Douglass, Volume 3: The Civil War, 1861–1865,* ed. Philip S. Foner. New York: International Publishers, 1952.

Du Bois, W. E. Burghardt. *The Souls of Black Folk: Essays and Sketches.* Greenwich, CT: Fawcett Publications, 1961.

———. *The Suppression of the African Slave Trade to the United States of America, 1638–1870.* Baton Rouge: Louisiana State University Press, 1969.

———. *The Negro.* New York: Oxford University Press, 1970.

———. "The Souls of White Folk." In *W.E.B. Du Bois: A Reader,* ed. Meyer Weinberg. New York: Harper and Row, 1970.

———. "Prospect of a World Without Racial Conflict." In *W.E.B. Du Bois Speaks: Speeches and Addresses, 1920–1963,* ed. Philip S. Foner. New York: Pathfinder Press, 1970.

———. "The Negro and the Warsaw Ghetto." In *W.E.B. Du Bois Speaks: Speeches and Addresses, 1920–1963,* ed. Philip S. Foner. New York: Pathfinder Press, 1970.

———. "Disfranchisement." In *W.E.B. Du Bois Speaks: Speeches and Addresses, 1890–1919,* ed. Philip S. Foner. New York: Pathfinder Press, 1970.

Foner, Eric. "The New View of Reconstruction." *American Heritage* 34, no. 6 (October–November 1983): 10–15.

Franklin, John Hope. *Racial Equality in America.* Chicago: University of Chicago Press, 1976.

———. *The Color Line: Legacy for the Twenty-first Century.* Columbia: University of Missouri Press, 1993.

Gay, Peter. *The Cultivation of Hatred: The Bourgeois Experience, Victoria to Freud.* New York: W.W. Norton & Company, 1993.

Hacker, Andrew. *Two Nations: Black and White, Separate, Hostile, Unequal.* New York: Charles Scribner's Sons, 1992.

Haller, John S., Jr. *Outcasts from Evolution: Scientific Attitudes of Racial Inferiority, 1859–1900.* Urbana: University of Illinois Press, 1971.

Hallie, Philip P. *Cruelty,* rev. ed. Middletown, CT: Wesleyan University Press, 1982.

Heilbroner, Robert. *Visions of the Future: The Distant Past, Yesterday, To-day, and Tomorrow*. New York: Oxford University Press, 1995.

Herrnstein, Richard J., and Charles Murray. *The Bell Curve: Intelligence and Class Structure in American Life*. New York: Free Press, 1994.

Hofstadter, Richard. *The American Political Tradition and the Men Who Made It*. New York: Random House, 1974.

Horsman, Reginald. *Race and Manifest Destiny: The Origins of American Racial Anglo-Saxonism*. Cambridge, MA: Harvard University Press, 1981.

Huggins, Nathan Irvin. *Black Odyssey: The African-American Ordeal in Slavery*. New York: Random House, 1990.

Jean, Clinton M. *Behind the Eurocentric Veils: The Search for African Re-alities*. Amherst: University of Massachusetts Press, 1991.

Jenkins, Adelbert H. *The Psychology of the Afro-American: A Humanist Ap-proach*. New York: Pergamon Press, 1982.

Jewell, Sue K. *From Mammy to Miss America and Beyond: Cultural Images and the Shaping of U.S. Social Policy*. New York: Routledge, 1993.

Johannsen, Robert W. *Lincoln, the South and Slavery: The Political Dimen-sion*. Baton Rouge: Louisiana State University Press, 1991.

Kaufman, Alan S. *Intelligent Testing with the WISC-R*. New York: John Wiley & Sons, 1979.

Kovel, Joel. *White Racism: A Psychohistory*. New York: Columbia University Press, 1984.

Landry, Bert. *The New Black Middle Class*. Berkeley and Los Angeles: Uni-versity of California Press, 1987.

Lewis, Bernard. *Cultures in Conflict: Christians, Muslims, and Jews in the Age of Discovery*. New York: Oxford University Press, 1995.

Majors, Richard, and Janet Mancini Billson. *Cool Pose: The Dilemmas of Black Manhood in America*. New York: Maxwell Macmillan Inter-national, 1992.

Martin, Waldo E., Jr. *The Mind of Frederick Douglass*. Chapel Hill: Univer-sity of North Carolina Press, 1984.

Mensh, Elaine, and Harry Mensh. *The IQ Mythology: Class, Race, Gender, and Inequality*. Carbondale: Southern Illinois University Press, 1991.

Myrdal, Gunnar. *Challenge of Affluence*. New York: Pantheon Books, 1963.

Omi, Michael, and Howard Winant. *Racial Formation in the United States from the 1960s to the 1980s*. New York: Routledge & Kegan Paul, 1986.

Patterson, Orlando. *The Ordeal of Integration Progress and Resentment in America's "Racial" Crisis*. Washington, D.C.: Civitas Counterpoint, 1997.

Pieterse, Jan Nederveen. *White on Black: Images of Africa and Blacks in*

Western Popular Culture. New Haven, CT: Yale University Press, 1992.

Richardson, Ken. *Understanding Intelligence*. Philadelphia: Open University Press, 1991.

Schlesinger, Arthur, Jr. *The Disuniting of America: Reflections on a Multicultural Society*. New York: W.W. Norton & Company, 1992.

Sharp, Evelyn. *The IQ Cult*. New York: Coward, McCann & Geohaegan, 1972.

Sigelman, Lee, and Susan Welch. *Black Americans' Views of Racial Inequality: The Dream Deferred*. New York: Cambridge University Press, 1991.

Steele, Shelby. *The Content of Our Character*. New York: St. Martin's Press, 1990.

Thomas, Alexander, and Samuel Sillen. *Racism and Psychiatry*. New York: Brunner/Mazel, 1972.

Tucker, Robert C. "Stalinism as Revolution from Above." In *Stalinism: Essays in Historical Interpretation*, ed. Robert C. Tucker. New York: W.W. Norton & Company, 1977.

Walton, John. *Sociology and Critical Inquiry: The Work, Tradition, and Purpose*, 2nd. ed. Belmont, CA: Wadsworth Publishing Company, 1990.

Watson, Harry L. *Liberty and Power: The Politics of Jacksonian America*. New York: Noonday Press, 1990.

West, Cornel. *Prophetic Fragments*. Grand Rapids, MI: William B. Eerdmans Publishing Company, 1988.

———. *Race Matters*. Boston: Beacon Press, 1993.

Wilhelm, Sidney M. *Who Needs the Negro?* Cambridge, MA: Schenkman Publishing, 1970.

Williams, Patricia J. *The Rooster's Egg*. Cambridge, MA: Harvard University Press, 1995.

Wilson, William Julius. *The Declining Significance of Race: Blacks and Changing American Institutions*, 2nd. ed. Chicago: University of Chicago Press, 1980.

———. *The Truly Disadvantaged: The Inner City, the Underclass, and Public Policy*. Chicago: University of Chicago Press, 1987.

Woodward, C. Vann. *The Strange Career of Jim Crow*. 3d. rev. ed. New York: Oxford University Press, 1974.

Wright, W. D. "The Faces of Racism." *Western Journal of Black Studies* 2, no. 4 (1987): 168–76.

Index

About the Author

W. D. WRIGHT is Professor of History at Southern Connecticut State University. He is the author of *Black Intellectuals, Black Cognition, and a Black Aesthetic* (Praeger, 1997).

ISBN 0-275-96197-4

90000>

EAN

9 780275 961978

HARDCOVER BAR CODE